Memoirs of a Dervish

Memoirs of a Dervish

ROBERT IRWIN

P
PROFILE BOOKS

First published in Great Britain in 2011 by
PROFILE BOOKS LTD
3A Exmouth House
Pine Street
Exmouth Market
London EC1R 0JH
www.profilebooks.com

1 3 5 7 9 10 8 6 4 2

Typeset in Sabon by MacGuru Ltd
info@macguru.org.uk
Printed and bound in Great Britain by
Clays, Bungay, Suffolk

A CIP catalogue record for this book is available from the British Library.

ISBN 978 1 86197 991 9
eISBN 978 1 84765 404 5

The paper this book is printed on is certified by the © 1996 Forest Stewardship
Council A.C. (FSC). It is ancient-forest friendly. The printer holds FSC chain of
custody SGS-COC-2061

FSC
Mixed Sources
Product group from well-managed
forests and other controlled sources
Cert no. SGS-COC-2061
www.fsc.org
© 1996 Forest Stewardship Council

To Helen, who rescued me from myself

The default setting of a memoir is yearning. Biography and autobiography tell the story of a life, but a memoir conjures a ghost image: the adventure missed, the love refused, the road not travelled, the might-have-beens. Perhaps memoir writing is itself a kind of adventure: a process as much of forming as describing.

Jane Shilling reviewing Luke Jennings's memoir *Blood Knots*
in the *Daily Telegraph*, 24 April 2010

CONTENTS

PREFACE

WHY DID I WRITE THIS BOOK? The causes are multiple. First, I badly wanted to create a work of literary art and perhaps also to give my youth a retrospective artistic shape. Then I wanted to know where I stood, both in relation to the mystical states I experienced as a young man and in relation to my eventual death and judgement. But I also wanted to give an account of Sufism from the inside, as well as instructing readers in the basic elements of Islam and the difficulties a Western convert is likely to face. At the same time I wanted to give an impression of how it felt to be young in the hippy sixties from the perspective of someone who was not part of the underground countercultural elite. In particular, I wanted to shed some light on the occult and mystical aspects of the counterculture, as well as some of the ludicrous and half-witted aspects of the hippy sixties. Additionally this is the story of someone who sat at the feet of a series of remarkable teachers. It is a book about teacher–student relations and, if Lynn Barber had not already taken the title for her excellent memoir, I might have called my book *An Education*.

There is a lot about dreams in this book, and it is – as Sigmund Freud might have put it – overdetermined. In Freud's *The Interpretation of Dreams*, a dream is said to be overdetermined if its plot and its various images are based on multiple causes. So in a dream the rocking horse in the corner of the attic may draw upon a glimpse of a rocking horse in a toyshop in the course of the previous day, but at the same time it may also allude to a deeply repressed child-hood trauma, conceivably something as serious as sexual molestation. A dream is compounded of many elements coming from different levels of the psyche and a success-ful interpretation requires understanding of the dream's images at several levels.

Over the decades my memories – my dreams – of the sixties coalesced into a kind of demon that lurked inside me. But I have found the writing of *Memoirs of a Dervish* to be a kind of exorcism. Something has been set free. I am not yet sure what.

1. The eighteenth-century Sufi Shaikh Ahmed Tijany

OXFORD

IT WAS IN MY FIRST YEAR at Oxford that I decided that I wanted to become a Muslim saint. I wish I could remember more. I do remember that early in the Hilary term of 1965, when it was still cold and there was snow on the ground, Ralph Davis, one of Merton's history tutors, set me to write an essay on the early Franciscan Order. I cannot recall what the title was, but I guess that I was being asked to judge the degree to which the original spirit and aims of St Francis were preserved as the order he had founded became increasingly institutionalised. The required reading consisted mostly of primary sources, medieval accounts of the saint's life. These included lives of St Francis by Thomas of Celano and St Bonaventure, as well as something called *The Little Flowers of St Francis*, which sounded as though it would be just soppy, but which turned out to be a fascinatingly astringent document.

To be studying the Middle Ages in such a medieval environment was a curious form of total immersion. Merton had been founded in 1264 and early members of the college had taken part in the great metaphysical debate between two famous Franciscan philosophers, Duns Scotus and William of Ockham. On the upper floor of the college's medieval library books bound in leather or vellum were still chained to the shelves. The grace before dinner was and is in Latin. The central part of the college is built around quadrangles and the stonework of the oldest buildings glows golden under the sun. Davis occupied a set of oak-panelled rooms in Fellows Quad and his tutorials were conducted like scholastic disputations. So that in each essay I was supposed to put forward a thesis to which in response he would propose a counter-thesis. It did not matter what I might argue; he would always have the counter-argument ready. He was the master of what looked like childishly simple-minded questions, but those questions were used to great effect in the demolition of undergraduate would-be sophistication.

The narrative of *The Little Flowers* ('Fioretti') teemed with miracles and acts of intense piety. St Francis almost went blind from weeping. He ate nothing but half a loaf of bread while fasting through Lent. He converted the wolf of Gubbio. At night he spoke with Christ in the woods and before his death he received the stigmata. But from almost the beginning there were also backbiting and execration. On one occasion the Devil possessed the body of an angry friar. The Devil also appeared in the guise of Christ to a certain Brother Ruffino and told him that he was damned. Brother Elia's pride and ambition were a great torment to St Francis and he 'knew in spirit that Brother Elia was damned and was to leave the Order'. As I struggled with my essay about the compromises that medieval mystics and ascetics had to make with more worldly people, I did not guess that I should soon be entering a very similar world and that the time of miracles was only months away. My future teachers in North Africa would instruct me in matters that were not on any university syllabus.

The subject of mysticism was a congenial one. Even before arriving in Oxford I had read *The Way of Zen* by Alan Watts and *Zen in the Art of Archery* by Eugen Herrigel. I read haikus by Bashō and tried composing some

2

myself. That kind of literature was part of the sixties noo-
sphere, or collective consciousness. I cannot remember
how I came across Buddhism while still a schoolboy, but
I guess that my interest in it was fuelled by my antipathy
towards school chapel services. At Epsom College there
was chapel every morning and twice on Sundays, with a
lengthy sermon on Sunday evening, as well as house prayers
every evening. Unless one was into fancying choirboys, and
I was not, there was nothing to disturb the torpid, joyless
and peculiarly English tedium of those prayers, hymns and
readings. I was at that time a militant atheist and had been
beaten by my housemaster for making a mockery of house
prayers. As I understood it, Buddhism was a religion for
atheists and one with the added attraction of exoticism.
Anyway, weeks after I arrived in Oxford I joined the Oxford
Buddhist Society. This proved to be a rather odd undergraduate group, as most of its members seemed to be much
more interested in anarchism, drugs and Sufism than they
were in Buddhism.

St Francis (1182–1226), the son of a wealthy businessman
in Assisi, chose to marry Lady Poverty. He renounced all
his property, including his clothes. 'If thou wilt be perfect,
go and sell that thou hast, and give to the poor' (Matthew
19:21). Kittoo, a wealthy Indian student I knew at Keble,
was to do the same thing. The affectation of poverty was an
important strain in the hippy style. When I was young, the
possible importance of class and social origins in mysticism
was not something I had given any thought to. But in 1978
Alexander Murray was to publish a remarkably original
work, *Reason and Society in the Middle Ages*. One of the
things Murray did was to go through *The Oxford History
of the Christian Church*, from which he drew out a list of
seventy-eight saints. Of these the social origins of seventy-
one could be determined: approximately sixty-two, that is
87 per cent, were of upper-class birth. Murray concluded

this particular chapter, which was devoted to the conspicuous piety of the nobility, by remarking that the 'adoption of an ascetic way of life by those who are not obliged to it has rarely failed to excite a certain wonder among those who see it'.

I have not kept the essay that I wrote for Davis on St Francis and the Franciscan Order, but I am sure that in my account of internal developments within the order, I made no reference to miracles, though it had been recorded that these happened frequently and they were sometimes deployed by St Francis and his disciples to confound their critics by demonstrating that God was on the side of the friar who had performed or at least witnessed the miracle. However, professional historians were supposed to ignore the miraculous in their analyses of the past. The miraculous never happened. The unspoken and condescending implication was that medieval people were peculiarly prone to hallucinations.

I was in a phase when I was reading novels not for pleasure, but in order to discover the Meaning of Life. Novels by Dostoevsky, Proust, Hermann Hesse or J. D. Salinger seemed more likely to provide the required answer than, say, novels by Austen, Dickens, Wodehouse or Ian Fleming. (I now think more highly of Austen and Wodehouse in this respect.) The idea that the Meaning of Life might be buried in a novel now strikes me as quite curious, but it was through reading Salinger's *Franny and Zooey* (1961) that I came across the Hesychastic autobiography-cum-devotional text *The Way of a Pilgrim*. In Salinger's novel, Franny is carrying 'a small pea-green cloth-bound book' when she steps off the train and into the arms of her boyfriend. Later in a restaurant it becomes apparent that she is bored with her boyfriend. After he has been monopolising the conversation for quite some time, he demands to know about the little green book. She tries to tell him:

'I mean it starts out with this peasant – the pilgrim – wanting to find out what it means in the Bible when it says you should pray incessantly. You know. Without stopping. In Thessalonians or someplace. So he starts out walking all over Russia, looking for somebody who can tell him *how* to pray incessantly. And what you should say if you do.'

But the boyfriend is more interested in dissecting the pair of frog's legs on his plate and Franny's attempt to impress him with the simple power of her book tails off. Towards the end of the meal she faints. After she comes round: 'Her lips began to move, forming soundless words, and they continued to move.'

In *The Way of a Pilgrim*, which is the book that Franny had been reading, the anonymous nineteenth-century Russian pilgrim tells how he came to embrace perpetual prayer as he walked through the countryside with only 'a knapsack with some dried bread in it on my back, and in a breast-pocket a Bible. And that is all.' Since the first Epistle of St Paul to the Thessalonians enjoins us to 'Pray without ceasing', that is what he did. He repeated 'Lord Jesus Christ have mercy on me' 3,000 times a day, until those words formed themselves again and again without any conscious volition and he was filled with perpetual joy. Having purchased a pea-green copy of *The Way of a Pilgrim* in Blackwell's Bookshop for thirteen shillings and sixpence, I read it at a sitting in the course of an afternoon and then, as darkness fell, I began to walk barefoot round and round St Alban's Quad, reciting 'Lord Jesus Christ have mercy on me', and so I continued all through the night, until the dawn chorus, when I gave up and went to bed, unenlightened and unimproved. I did not believe in God, but, allegedly, as Franny told her boyfriend, soon to be her ex-boyfriend, 'the marvellous thing is, when you first start doing it, you don't even have to have faith in what you're doing. I mean even if you're terribly embarrassed about the whole thing, it's perfectly alright.' I found the idea that religion works even for atheists and agnostics comforting.

I was a mad boy. I often went barefoot in those days. St Francis had gone barefoot and so, in more modern times, did Sandie Shaw. It had become a hippy thing, though I was at first suspicious of hippydom and preferred to think of myself as a beatnik. In my first term at Oxford someone pointed to a young man in dark glasses, black roll-neck pullover, jeans and sandals and said, 'He's a beatnik.' I looked at him and decided that I wanted to be a beatnik too, but I soon acquired a bigger ambition.

Outside the medieval walls of Merton the sixties were happening. I don't think that they actually started in 1960; 1964 was closer to the real start. Somewhere in his diaries, Alan Bennett remarks that the lasting damage to British society was not committed by the hairy evangelists of permissiveness, but was the work of the property developers. Despite the developers, there were still a few bomb sites in London. The sixties was an amazingly drab time really. Better Books in Charing Cross Road was selling books about mandalas, psychedelics and free love, but a few doors down there was still a shop displaying a wide range of surgical trusses in its window. The porters in Covent Garden wore cloth caps and the men who walked across Waterloo Bridge heading for the City mostly wore bowler hats. The majority of young men had short hair and many of them used Brylcreem. In the cities one still saw rag-and-bone men, lamplighters for the gas lamps and horse-drawn milk floats. Prawn cocktail was the height of gastronomic sophistication and there were few Indian restaurants in Britain. In the early sixties the television screens were dominated by people like Hughie Green and Lady Isobel Barnett and the record charts by Adam Faith, Marty Wilde and Cliff Richard. Though a lot was written about youth power, it was bogus. Old men governed the country, ran the businesses, commanded the troops and officiated as bishops. They always had and they always will.

One had to hunt for the hippy, psychedelic, mystic, flower-power sixties. It was to be found only in pockets of London and a few provincial outposts. The sixties scene, when one found it, was horridly meritocratic. To be really part of it one had to be young, beautiful, fluent and successful. I was only young. The decade has been retrospectively annexed by people like Richard Neville, Germaine Greer, Howard Marks, Felix Dennis, John Michell and Jeff Nuttall. These were people who were 'where it was all happening'. It was happening in Carnaby Street, the Arts Lab, Gandalf's Garden, Indica Bookshop, Middle Earth, the offices of *Oz* and the *International Times*. In Gandalf's Garden, a tea shop a long way down the King's Road, I met a man who had had his skull trepanned in Tibet. He was preaching to anyone who would listen that trepanning would help them become whatever they wanted to become. When he looked at me, I said that I wanted to become a playboy. He hesitated before affirming that trepanning would help with that too. In Carnaby Street I bought a silver shirt. I danced with a fey, blonde girlfriend at Middle Earth. I ate macrobiotic brown rice and drank peach tea at the Arts Lab and was part of the audience that lay on mattresses in its tiny cinema and watched experimental, erotic films like Jack Smith's *Flaming Creatures*. So I knew those places, but not well and I have a different story to tell.

There were hints of Paradise in the sixties – the beautiful young women, the enchanting music, the drugs, the incense, the swirling bright colours. But mostly I stood outside the gates of Paradise looking in. I matriculated at Oxford in October 1964. I still do not really know what 'matriculated' means, but roughly it meant the start of undergraduate life. This was a bit like being under a starter's gun.

The glittering prizes were a few decades in the future. I nervously surveyed the confident young men and women in the streets and lecture halls. It was a betting certainty that among them were future prime ministers, celebrated actors, cabinet undersecretaries, award-winning newspaper columnists and novelists. But who were they? There was an elite society for Mertonians called the Myrmidons. I was not invited to join, nor did I dare speak at the Oxford Union or audition for the Oxford University Dramatic Society. I was not aware of something called the Bullingdon Club. People who have been to public school are supposed to be sophisticated and they are often resented as such by people who come to Oxbridge from state schools. But I had arrived at Oxford an almost complete barbarian, for, not only had I almost no experience in talking to girls, I was also unused to drink and I left my first Oxford sherry party crawling on my hands and knees.

In an essay entitled 'On Being Conservative', the political philosopher Michael Oakeshott wrote:

> Everybody's young days are a dream, a delightful insanity, a sweet solipsism. Nothing in them has a fixed shape, nothing a fixed price; everything is a possibility, and we live happily on credit. There are no obligations to be observed; there are no accounts to be kept ... The world is a mirror in which we seek the reflection of our own desires.

Yes, all that is true, but ... in the sixties I was young, fit and lean, with everything before me. Though I am none of these things now, I have no desire to return to my previous state, for I was also lonely, unconfident, sex-starved and somewhat mad. Lonely in my oak-panelled, chilly room, I was reluctant to acknowledge the sad necessity of living in a body and, having read P. D. Ouspensky on the subject, I spent hours lying on the floor trying to get my astral self to lift itself out of my physical body and drift up to the ceiling. (Ouspensky (1878–1947) was an esoteric philosopher of Russian origin who wrote strange books on time, other dimensions and heightened awareness.) Alternatively, I struggled to get a pencil to levitate. I had my record player for company and listened again and again to Françoise Hardy's song, with its opening, '*Tous les garçons et les filles de mon age se promènent dans la rue, deux par deux, et les mains dans les mains ...*' and its plaintive refrain, '*Oui, mais moi je vais seule.*' Hardy preceded Jean Shrimpton as my pin-up. But now that I am in my personal sixties, no music has more power to evoke those cold, sixties winters spent hunched by a two-bar electric fire with a mug of instant coffee than recordings of the Scottish folk singer Bert Jansch's bleak guitar solos. Threads of incense and cigarette smoke twisted themselves around the melancholy lyrics. I was lonely and fearful and also bored. When was life going to start? God knows why but, as I have already mentioned, I had an ambition. I wanted to become a saint.

2. Joseph, Pharaoh and Pharaoh's wife

2

ODD PEOPLE

I SPENT MOST OF THE SIXTIES reading and dreaming. Ever since my first year at boarding school I had kept a record of my dreams and, in my final year, this was expanded into a series of sporadic diaries, and these diaries continued on throughout the sixties. In one of the rooms I had in Merton I rigged up a notice that was suspended on threads from the ceiling over my pillow, so that it was the first thing I saw when I opened my eyes in the morning. It read NOW YOU ARE AWAKE, REMEMBER YOUR DREAMS. In my notebooks night-time visions continued for a long time to take precedence over the record of daily realities, but eventually the diurnal diaries took over. So many scrawled pages of self-obsession, pretension and naivety make painful reading today and I have turned to them with reluctance. Yet I have to, for my memory of those times is so bad – like a poorly preserved silent film featuring people whose faces are blurred or even non-existent, together with voiceless conversations and abrupt jumps in continuity. My memory tells me stories. It always pretends to be telling true stories, but sometimes it lies to me, as it seeks to artistically shape my life and provide a founding myth of my identity.

For some daft reason I did not date my diaries. Worse, I had an unerring instinct for omitting to record the really interesting things that were going on around me as I crazily struggled to turn introspection into a philosophical tool. In so doing, I failed to register what turns of phrase, visual styles and social conventions were doomed to vanish in future years. Despite being a keen reader of science fiction, I had no sense of how much things were going to change in the decades to come. (By the way, if one followed the blue-prints for the future as outlined by sixties science fiction, by now we should have glass-domed colonies on Mars and waiter service performed by robots, but no laptops.) Surprisingly often my memory and my diaries flatly contradict one another and I remain uncertain as to which is the less reliable. A diary for 1965 tells me that I practised fire-swallowing. Unfortunately I have no memory of this. Disturbing doodles run down the margins of my diaries. As I read them now, they were written by a rather boring though pitiable stranger. I strove to be aphoristic. I was also capable of such fatuities as 'I agree with Wittgenstein on this.' I had hoped that I was bottling time, but the stuff of time just trickled away. Time is pretty strange anyway. Apparently the Hopi Indians believe that every day is the same day. It is just that different things happen in it.

Redmond O'Hanlon remembers that when he first met me I was standing on my head with my legs in the full lotus position. (Yoga was something else I dabbled in.) Though O'Hanlon has found fame as a travel writer, none of the undergraduates I knew at Oxford became prime minister or a cabinet undersecretary or a famous actor. Yet slowly I did get to know other students. It seemed that in the early sixties every secondary school in Britain nurtured at least one boy or girl who had embraced pacifism or anarchism or both, studied Zen, practised divination from tarot cards, and read J. D. Salinger and Hermann Hesse, and then Oxford gathered these weirdos up and distributed them around its colleges.

In the course of my first year, I enlisted in a series of overlapping gangs of intellectuals, amateur metaphysicians, *soi-disant* anarchists, would-be mystics, potheads and eccentrics. We thought that we were never going to die. Even so there was a lot of talk about the Angel of Death. It was rumoured that one in five had seen this Angel. He appeared before your bed and as he got successively closer to the bed the closer you were to death. Though it was wild fun at the time, the years that followed were to take their toll on these, my new friends; one or two committed suicide, half a dozen spent time in the Warneford Hospital (previously known as the Radcliffe Lunatic Asylum), one jumped off Folly Bridge into shallow water and was consequently paralysed from the waist down, another died of a drug overdose and another entered a closed order of nuns. Yet another, as I shall relate, died of pneumonia in a Sufi monastery. Many others, most I guess, eventually gave up being weird, took their degrees and found regular paid employment. Anyway, by about halfway through the second term, I could no longer reckon myself to be lonely. Not all my friends were nice, but then I preferred interesting to nice. Troops of strange young men and women regularly turned up in my room and stayed to debate the Meaning of Life, the rules of the cosmic game, the burgeoning power of the police state, the correct Zen way of making tea and suchlike matters. The debates were leisurely and a kind of tradition developed of not adjourning until we had heard the beginnings of the dawn chorus.

The Meaning of Life came up rather a lot. I remember John Aczel shouting, 'Who will tell me the Meaning of Life? I will jump up and touch the ceiling for him.' From the perspective of youth it was obvious that one should not get much older before one discovered the Meaning of Life. Otherwise, how could one live it properly? But it was not obvious what the procedure was for discovering the Meaning of Life. We heard rumours that there was a Meaning of Life clinic in Bulgaria. I was pale and thin and my hands shook from unfocused intensity. 'To burn always with this hard, gem-like flame, to maintain this ecstasy, is success in life.' Although I do not think that any of us had read Walter Pater's Victorian take on the Renaissance, many of my contemporaries took his injunction for granted. For us, intensity had an independent value. Everything was absolute. We talked often about suicide, or, more rarely, murder. One of my strange new friends described carrying a knife and following a man through the fog for a mile or more, meditating on whether to kill this complete stranger or not. 'Kill a man. He who has killed a man sleeps easily' was painted on the wall of his bedroom. Peter Fuller (of whom more later) talked frequently about the desirability of killing someone. When we were very bored, we placed five-pound notes on the bars of my electric fire and watched them burn. This was something that we had picked up, appropriately enough, from *The Idiot* by Dostoevsky. Dostoevsky and Wittgenstein were the prophets of intensity. We played cruel truth games, for what was the point of the old bourgeois courtesies that were nothing better than lies?

Everybody, including me, seemed to be writing bad poetry. On 11 June 1965 a gang of us squeezed into a van, which had the words *Luxe, volupté, bonté* painted in lurid lettering on one of its sides, and we drove down to London to attend the International Poetry Incarnation at the Albert Hall – one of the iconic events of sixties counterculture. I was there with Peter Fuller, Jenny (his then girlfriend) and Kittoo. I wandered around in a cape and brandished a silver-topped cane. The event was crowded, chaotic and druggy. Michael Horovitz, Adrian Mitchell, Allen Ginsberg, Gregory Corso and Lawrence Ferlinghetti were among the poets who performed. 'World declaration hot peace shower! Earth's grass is free! Cosmic poetry! Visitation accidentally happening casually! Spontaneous planet-chant Carnival! Mental cosmonaut poet epiphany, immaculate supranational Poesy insemination!' (I can sense the lack of confidence in the prose.) I thought Ferlinghetti was obscure, Horovitz childish and sententious, Adrian Mitchell rather cracker-barrel. But I admired Anselm Hollo, Ernst Jandl, George Macbeth and Ginsberg. Still, on the whole, the poets did not make much impression on me, but the audience did. Hitherto, I had not realised how many long-haired, doped, garishly attired freaks there were in Britain. We were the coming storm.

A counterculture was developing but, since it was Oxford, it was definitely a bookish one. It was also uncritically eclectic. The sixties generation was one whose thinking had been done for it in advance. As part of my preparation for becoming a beatnik, I of course read Jack Kerouac, author of the key beat novel, *On the Road*. Kerouac had written of 'a generation of crazy illuminated hipsters suddenly rising and roaming America, serious, curious, bumming and hitchhiking everywhere, ragged beatific, beautiful in an ugly graceful new way – a vision gleaned from the way we had heard the word *beat* meaning down and out but full of intense conviction'. Yes, having read that, I wanted to hitchhike, but to do it *intensely*. It was a shock when, years later, I came across photos of Kerouac, Neal Cassady and other beats. They looked really straight, for they wore check shirts and had short hair. I also learned that Kerouac spent most of his time living with his mother. (One gets a similar sort of jolt from seeing group photographs of the Surrealists in the thirties. There they all are in jackets and ties with neatly parted hair. What kind of '*dérèglement de tous les sens*' could have been going on then?)

But it was not long before I realised that I was too late

to join the beats and that my true destiny was to become a hippy, if only a part-time one. Again, initially it meant reading a different set of books from the ones straight people read. 'I have been a stranger in a strange land' (Exodus, 2:22). This verse from the Bible provided the title for a science fiction novel by Robert Heinlein. *Stranger in a Strange Land* (1961) was a cult book for many of my friends, though Heinlein (1907–88) was an improbable guru of the hippy sixties, as he was a mainstream American science fiction writer, a war veteran, a patriot, a hawk for the Vietnam War and a populist and most of his novels featured tough men of action. *Starship Troopers* (1959), one of his best-known novels, has a militarist plot tending even towards fascism, and its themes were in all respects repellent to hippy thinking. Yet *Stranger in a Strange Land*, on the other hand, became a kind of bible to the hippies, druggies and squatters of the sixties.

Valentine Michael Smith, who has been raised on Mars by Martians and has acquired psi powers in the course of his education, arrives on Earth. He can make people and things discorporate, or vanish, into another dimension. He lets himself be killed by a mob and discorporates himself, so vanishing from a planet still riddled with the traditional prejudices. Smith is an innocent, Christ-like figure (somewhat reminiscent of Dostoevsky's idiot, Prince Myshkin). During his time on Earth he presides over water-sharing ceremonies and sessions of free love and he teaches people how to grok. To grok is to directly intuit and fully understand the essence of a person or thing, without recourse to tedious rationality. Heinlein's opinionated, preachy novel attacked property, monogamy and conventional religion. The blurb of the first British edition described it as 'a searing indictment of Western civilization'. It is a rebellious fantasy of wish fulfilment which played on my adolescent longing to grow up as a messiah with superpowers.

Oxford potheads sat around grokking one another and a few even re-enacted water ceremonies. It was all very gentle and went well with Donovan on the record player. I think that part of what one was supposed to be grokking was vibes. Vibes were everywhere. People emanated them and on hashish one could become very sensitive to other people's bad vibes. Also some of the people on the scene used to go around vampiristically drinking other people's psychic energy. I am still unclear exactly how this was done.

Paranoia was also an intrinsic part of drug culture in the sixties and it probably still is today. Inevitably there was paranoia about 'the fuzz' (the police) and the likelihood of an imminent bust, but there also seemed to be a paranoiac ingredient in the drugs themselves. The drugs made one doubt one's surroundings and the people in them. I remember walking in on a friend who was tripping on LSD. Although I did not realise it, I was within an inch of being knifed, as he had identified me (black pullover, black jeans and dark glasses) as the Antichrist. Then there was also paranoia about the quality of the drugs one was taking and, if one was having a bad trip, then it was reasonable, or at least it seemed reasonable, to suspect that the stuff one had bought had been laced with something else.

Kingsley Amis once observed that 'the golden age of science fiction is twelve'. I encountered science fiction somewhat earlier, having read *Kemlo and the Gravity Rays* at the age of ten. (It was in my Christmas stocking and I finished it before breakfast.) I moved on to the Edgar Rice Burroughs's Barsoom sequence of novels, *A Princess of Mars*, *The Gods of Mars*, *The Warlords of Mars* and so on, most of which I borrowed from the Boots circulating subscription library. In the course of Burroughs's heroic cycle, John Carter won the hand of the egg-laying princess

Dejah Thoris. When my mother went shopping in Guild-ford at the weekend she used to dump my brother and me at the children's matinee cinema. We felt dumped and hated it. The cinema retained an organist whom we and the rest of the children pelted with whatever we could muster and I can remember the manager coming out to remonstrate with us. As often as not, the feature film starred Norman Wisdom, for whom I developed a fierce loathing which persists to this day. No man should have to base his career on cringing, or the simulation of it. However, the cinema also showed shorter episodes of *Flash Gordon*. The women, Dale Arden and Princess Aura, who was the daughter of Ming the Merciless, were clad in what looked like shiny silk and showed a lot of leg and, for me, this was the first faint bat squeak of sexuality.

Science fiction admonished its readers to marvel at creation and, as I was soon to discover, this was a theme that had been anticipated by the Qur'an (*Sura* 55):

> *All that dwells upon the earth is perishing, yet still*
> *Abides the Face of thy Lord, majestic, splendid.*
> *O which of your Lord's bounties will you and you deny?*
> *Whatsoever is in the heavens and the earth implore Him;*
> *Every day He is upon some labour.*
> *O which of your Lord's bounties will you and you deny?*

Science fiction works hard with paradoxes. Time travel allows the possibility that a man might become his own grandfather. A benighted traveller might find himself inhabiting a space that is essentially a Möbius strip or a world that is hyperboloid rather than spherical. Paradoxes of the infinite are staple in science fiction. Islamic mysticism, I discovered, is similarly paradox-ridden and obsessed with the infinite. Consider 'The lovers of God are concealed from Him by their very love', or Abu Yazid al-Bistami's 'For thirty years I sought for God, but when I paused to think He was the seeker and I the sought.' These days I no longer read science fiction. I have lost the capacity to be astounded and I am sad about that.

One afternoon in Guildford Public Library a title caught my eye – *The Three Stigmata of Palmer Eldritch* (1965). How was it possible to resist such a title? Its author, the American science-fiction writer Philip K. Dick (1928–82), was the unchallenged master of fantastic, druggy, paranoid literature. Far more than Heinlein, Dick was an obviously suitable guru for the sixties, since he was a drug-taking paranoiac with religious obsessions. To paraphrase Philip Larkin, paranoia was to Dick what daffodils were to Wordsworth. Dick was an offbeat product of the Californian counterculture, which, of course, was pretty offbeat in its own right. He was a prolific hack writer of genius. In his stories things were never what they seemed and there were conspiracies to manipulate reality, alternative universes hidden within the reality that one thought one was inhabiting and people who, on closer examination, turned out not to be people at all. The typical Dick novel, and he wrote a lot, was soaked in drugs.

Dick offered nightmares from which one could never awake. *The Three Stigmata of Palmer Eldritch* is about Chew-Z, a drug which destroys reality. The marketing slogan for Chew-Z was 'God promises eternal life. We can deliver it.' Palmer Eldritch becomes an evil Gnostic Christ figure in a drugs-generated universe and those who take his drug find themselves turning into him – that is, into a horrible version of God. W. S. Gilbert, the librettist of *HMS Pinafore*, *The Yeomen of the Guard* and similar operettas, was a big influence on Dick. The two writers shared a taste for preposterous plotting, an underlying pessimism and, above all, an obsessive delight in paradox. Dick was wonderfully and carelessly fertile with barmy ideas. His novels spoke to me, for when I looked around me, I could not quite believe that what you see is what you get. All the same, Dick's prose style was poor. I was reading him at the same time that I was reading Proust. It was difficult to compare the two and, as the infinitely wise Kai Lung observed in Ernest Bramah's story 'The Incredible Obtuseness of Those Who Had Opposed the Virtuous Kai Lung', 'How is it possible to suspend topaz in one cup of the balance and weigh it against amethyst in the other; or who in a single language can compare the tranquillizing grace of a maiden with the invigorating pleasure of witnessing a well-contested rat-fight?'

Dick's pulp fictions helped fuel a craze for godgames among my contemporaries. I set out a version of a godgame in a short-lived (single-issue), cyclostyled Oxford poetry magazine called *Speak One*. It began: 'In the beginning was the Great Gambler, and out of the primordial chaos he conceived the game of Chess. He created an infinite chequerboard, which he called the world: for seven days he meditated on a partner for the great Gamble, and finally came upon Himself; and he played the game with the infinite number of his Attributes' ... etc., etc. and *sic*. 'The First Illusion of Existence is that men do not realise that they are pawns in the great Game. Also the great Gambler is his own Illusion.' I published this tripe under the cringe-making pseudonym Kismet Gitano. In my defence, my friends were producing vaguely similar tripe.

The cosmic game was pretty much the same as the godgame. I wrote a lot of drivel about it in my diaries, like, for example, this: 'Any cosmic system in which one seeks to know may justly be regarded in the game image framework. If however the idea is simply to win out in existence, then the game may well be an invalid image, for the rule structure may not apply. In assimilation and knowledge it will do so.' My diaries are full of this wretched stuff. The godgame craze fed off science fiction, but it also owed something to Wittgenstein and his ideas about language as a series of language games and his conviction that certain philosophical questions, such as 'What is truth?', were no more than forms of wordplay. Additionally, a third-hand knowledge of Hinduism showed us that the world was *maya*, or illusion. The television series *The Prisoner*, which was shown in the years 1967–8, was yet a further source of godgame obsession, as its episodes featured paranoid fantasy, drugs, mind control and dream manipulation. The character played by Patrick McGoohan, christened by his captors as 'Number Six', constantly strove but failed to discover who Number One was.

Cardinal Newman wrote in *Apologia pro Vita Sua* (1864), looking back on his boyhood: 'I used to wish the Arabian Tales were true; my imagination ran on unknown influences, on magical powers and talismans. I thought life might be a dream, or I an Angel, and all this world a deception, my fellow angels by a playful device concealing themselves from me, and deceiving me with the semblance of the material world.'

I was hoping that once I had attained a certain level of awareness then I would be contacted by the players of the godgame, the Hidden Masters, the masters of the Glass Bead game, or whoever. *The Glass Bead Game* is of course the title of Hermann Hesse's novel. Hesse's books peddled a watered-down version of Indian philosophy. He made a cult of youth and presented the life ahead of youth as a spiritual journey.

Unusually, the protagonist of his novel *Steppenwolf* (published in German in 1927, but only translated in 1965), Harry Haller, was pretty old, for he was forty-eight. He judges his life to have been a failure and plans to commit suicide when he reaches fifty. However, an encounter with an initiatrix called Hermine leads him to the MAGIC

THEATRE. NOT FOR EVERYBODY; FOR MADMEN ONLY and a new life. As Gary Lachman noted in *Turn Off Your Mind: The Mystic Sixties and the Dark Side of the Age of Aquarius*, in the course of this novel, 'Haller smokes hashish and opium, sniffs cocaine, sleeps with a prostitute and learns the Fox Trot'. This is an interesting list of things to do. I have yet to learn the fox trot. The novel's antepenultimate sentence is: 'One day I would be a better hand at the game.' Hesse's novels appeared to offer wisdom, but years later a friend of mine pointed out that, from what we know of his life, Hesse ended up an embittered failure.

I had come to Hesse via the notes to T. S. Eliot's *The Waste Land*, which referred to another book by Hesse, *Glimpse into Chaos*. The annotation of *The Waste Land* effectively presented me and some of my contemporaries with an educational programme in which we were introduced not only to Hesse, but to Buddhism, the mysteries of the pentangle, ancient fertility rituals, tarot cards and Gérard de Nerval's poetry. I could go on about sixties reading matter: *Doctor Strange* comics, Colin Wilson's *The Outsider*, René Daumal's *Mount Analogue*, Louis Pauwels and Jacques Bergier's *The Dawn of Magic*, David Lindsay's *Voyage to Arcturus*, William Burroughs's *Dead Fingers* and much more.

There was a lot of talk by me and my contemporaries of writing a novel about Oxford, but none of us ever did. The talk about it was a feeble attempt to make one sound more interesting than one really was. I think I had the daft belief that unhappiness was a sufficient qualification for writing a novel. Andrew Sinclair's Cambridge novel *My Friend Judas* (1959), which I had read a few months before going up, captured some of the flavour of Oxbridge at that time. Its sad narrative of emotional betrayal and academic failure presaged the final outcome of my time in Oxford.

But enough of books, for the time being at least.

I became a collector of strange states of mind and I started a card index on this subject. I had entries for nausea, *kayf*, angst, *Gemutlichkeit*, *Sehnsucht*, fugitive awareness and various Zen levels of awareness, as well as déjà vu, presque vu and jamais vu. The experience of déjà vu, in which one has the sense that one has already experienced what one is now experiencing, hinted that the even, forward flow of time was not what it seemed to be. Presque vu was most tantalising, as it seemed to offer a fleeting version of absolute truth. Dostoevsky's idiot, Prince Myshkin, used to have such flashes of ultimate insight immediately prior to his epileptic fits. In the case of jamais vu, things that are normally part of one's world suddenly seem alien and utterly beyond interpretation. They exist without meaning or context. I once was gazing at some stones that formed part of the wall of Merton College and found myself incapable of understanding what I was seeing. The stones appeared as flat, flaky sponges. They might have been things from another planet. A sort of jamais vu can be deliberately achieved by repeating a phrase or a word to oneself a few thousand times. After a while, a word like 'dog' comes to lose all meaning and can no longer have reference to any-thing that one knows. But déjà vu and presque vu, like involuntary memory, cannot be deliberately stimulated. For me at that time it was mostly *Sehnsucht*, an unfocused yearning, that predominated. I did not know it, but I guess that what I yearned for was to encounter a woman and truly know her.

Hypnagogia and eidetic imagery (the two seem to shade into one another) was another thing that interested me. Hypnagogic images are ones that some people see on their eyelids before they drift off into sleep, but I can see them at any time of day or night. If I am in a dark room, or if I close my eyes, then I see images: faces, figures, buildings, forests, writings, beasts, seas and machines, and all of these things and more, in ceaseless movement and mutating into one another. I usually go to sleep while watching this chaotic Surrealist cinema. Just occasionally these days I hear snatches of hypnagogic speech, but when I was a child I used to have regular conversations with the creatures of my inner world. Emily Brontë, Charles Dickens, Robert Louis Stevenson and Richard Wagner tapped into hypnagogia. In an appendix to *Mysticism, Sacred and Profane*, R. C. Zaehner describes a specialised manifestation of hypnagogia:

> When dozing or falling asleep, I frequently saw faces forming in front of me. These faces are usually dimly lit against a black ground: they form, stay for a few seconds, and then disappear. As one face disappears, another slowly takes its place and disappears in its turn, and so on. These faces are usually of one type (old or middle-aged women, less frequently men, practically never young men or women, never children). These faces are never familiar.

(More on Zaehner shortly.) Most children enjoy hypnagogic imagery, but by the time they reach adulthood, the facility is usually lost. I was surprised eventually to learn that most of the people I knew had no idea what I was talking about when I asked them about their experience of hypnagogia, and this reminds me of the mother of a friend of mine who used to wake up every morning to a vision of 'the golden land'. It was years before she learned that not everybody did so.

It was my membership of the Oxford Buddhist Society that led me to Islam, though not straight away. In the early days I attended a lecture by Chögyam Thongpa Rinpoche. He had fled Tibet when the Chinese invaded in the fifties and studied in India before arriving in Oxford on a scholarship in 1963. Thongpa spoke of how a cloud had enveloped the Dalai Lama and allowed him to evade his Chinese pursuers and enter India. I meditated with Lama Thongpa and he chanted sutras while I sat cross-legged and tried (in vain, of course) to think of nothing at all. But I did learn how to use chopsticks from some of his Tibetan companions. Eventually, after his years in Oxford, Thongpa cast off the guise of a holy monk, slept with several of his female disciples and took up cocaine and alcohol consumption on a grand scale. He was to die of cirrhosis of the liver, while yet preserving something of the aura of a holy man.

Sangharakshita, the founder of Friends of the Western Buddhist Order, was another who came to speak to the Oxford Buddhist Society. He was British by birth and in the forties he had deserted from the army and gone to India to seek ordination as a Buddhist monk. He had a brilliant mind and he was an incisive speaker: 'Nirvana, the goal. Why do we seek it? When we know, we shall have achieved it. When we know why we think of it in the terms that we do, then we shall have it – when the pain of *samsara* seems to us as the bliss of nirvana.' Many years later, when the Ayatollah Khomeini had issued his fatwa decreeing that Salman Rushdie must die and the furore was at its height, I heard Sangharakshita being interviewed on the radio. He was asked what the Buddhist attitude to blasphemy was. His reply, if I remember correctly, was, 'We think blasphemy is a good thing for it forces the believer to think about his beliefs.' This seems to me an excellent approach to the issue. Christmas Humphreys, who was a senior figure among the Buddhist converts in London, also came to talk to us, but, since he was also a prosecuting QC who had been responsible for sending several people, including Ruth Ellis, to the gallows, we gave him a hard time. I found Buddhism interesting, but it also seemed rather bloodless, abstract and solipsistic.

We were hardly more than children. It was hard for us to put our toys away and it was perhaps natural for us to think of life as one big game. But according to the Qur'an: 'Do not think that We have created the world as a sport and plaything.' It was another undergraduate at Merton, Harvey, who introduced me to Islam and the mystical movement within Islam that is Sufism. I met him in the winter of 1964–5. He was then the leading figure in the Oxford Anarchist Society and also prominent in the Oxford Buddhist Society. But he was already a Muslim and had been given the name Ahmed when he converted. He was a charismatic figure with a leonine head of hair and looked like a dervish who had stepped out of an illustration to the *Arabian Nights*. Indeed, his maths tutor once reported to the college on Harvey's poor progress in that subject: 'Over the course of the year his appearance has increasingly come to resemble that of someone in the *Arabian Nights* and his concept of what constitutes an honest day's work seems to be drawn from the same source.' At the end of his first year Harvey switched to Arabic, a language for which he found no real aptitude. His poor progress in Arabic notwithstanding, I think that he is the most intelligent person I have met in my whole life. I always used to argue with Harvey, even though I had no real expectation of winning the argument. It was rather that I favoured an adversarial approach to understanding anything. So initially I spent many hours trying to demolish Harvey's attachment to Sufism and yet, at the same time, the conviction was growing within me that Sufism must be true.

As a schoolboy Harvey nursed the ambition of becoming a juvenile master criminal. But then thoughts of the dreadful punishments that might await him in the afterlife began to haunt him. So he started going to libraries in order to research the world's religions and discover which one offered the surest chance of salvation. In the end he decided that it must be Islam, as Christian doctrine seemed to be just too untidy. I think that it was the Swiss religious thinker Frithjof Schuon's book *The Transcendent Unity of Religions* (1953) that persuaded Harvey of this. Improbably it had turned up on the shelves of Chester-field Public Library. That book, like the rest of Schuon's prolific writings, is difficult, metaphysical and I would say somewhat arrogant in style. Although Schuon was a convert to Islam, he had gone on to teach a Perennialist doctrine that, at their highest level, Christianity, Islam, Judaism and Vedanta are the same religion and embody an ancient wisdom, but that this can only be appreciated by a Gnostic elite. As a student I used to take Schuon seri-ously. I now think that his writings are pernicious rubbish and that the tradition his disciples claim to represent is an invented one.

Having read Schuon at the age of twelve and being impressed by his argument that it did not matter which religion you followed so long as it was a traditional one, at fifteen Harvey converted to Islam and gave a talk about his conversion at Woking Mosque. By then, however, he had discovered Sufism, the inner heart of Islam. What is Sufism? The short (but misleading) answer is that Sufism is Islamic mysticism. A Sufi is a dervish is a *faqir* (*faqir* liter-ally means poor man; 'dervish' is a Persian word in origin). Although there is a lot of Western academic literature on the debt that Sufism owes to Christian asceticism, Neopla-tonism, Gnosticism, Buddhism and Hinduism, there is a good case to be made for Sufism being at the heart of Islam from its origin, for the tenets of Sufism are certainly there in the Qur'an. The verses found in *Sura* 24, *Nur* (Light), are mystical:

God is the light of the heavens and the earth;
The likeness of His light is as a niche
Wherein is a lamp
(The lamp in a glass,
The glass as it were a glittering star)
Kindled from a Blessed Tree,
An olive that is neither of the East nor of the West
Whose oil well nigh would shine, even if no fire touched it;
Light upon light;
(God guides to His light whom he will.)

So is:

We indeed created man; and We know
What his soul whispers within him,
And We are closer to him than the jugular vein.

So is:

Whithersoever you turn, there is the Face of God.

So is:

Nearer to thee and nearer
Then nearer to thee and nearer!

The first Sufis were individuals who lived solitary, ascetic lives. But in the late Middle Ages Sufi orders came into being, among them the Mevlevi or Whirling Dervishes, the Rifa'i or Howling Dervishes, the Naqshabandis, the Chistis, the Darqawis and the Sanussis. They met to pray, meditate, sing and dance in buildings that were variously known as *zawiya*s, *tekke*s or *ribat*s. Many Sufis sought a closer relationship with God than conventional Islam allowed. They sought annihilation before the Face of God. But though

3. Shaikh Ahmad al-'Alawi, the founder of the order

Sufism is often defined as Islamic mysticism, one does not have to be a mystic to be a Sufi. One only has to join a Sufi *tariqa* (literally 'way', but in this context meaning 'order'). I came to know people who had become Sufis for social or political reasons. They were good people, but not especially spiritual. Over the centuries the contribution of the Sufis to Islamic society and culture has been immense, particularly in the fields of literature and music.

But that winter I had no such synoptic view of the evolution of Sufism. Instead, over mugs of Blend 37 Instant Coffee, I was listening to strange tales about one particular *zawiya*, or Sufi centre, in Algeria that Harvey had first visited in 1963, and then returned to with his girlfriend, Anne Lindgren, in the summer of 1964. Harvey had learned about this *zawiya* through reading a remarkable book, *A Moslem Saint of the Twentieth Century: Shaikh Ahmad al-'Alawi*, by Martin Lings. Lings, who was Keeper of Oriental Books and Manuscripts in the British Museum, had written a moving account of the life and writings of an Algerian Sufi. As the book's blurb put it: 'For those who place the spiritual above the temporal and who are prepared to accept the validity of a religion other than their own, then Shaikh al-'Alawi must rank with Shri Ramana Maharishi of Tiruvannamalai as one of the truly great men of the century.' By the way, *A Moslem Saint of the Twentieth Century* is not a boring book. But most books on mysticism are mind-numbingly boring. They deal in abstractions, they are awash with technical terms, and all humanity is leached out as the authors drone on about levels of enlightenment, chakra centres and the paradoxes of the ultimate Oneness. Also, a lot of the books about mysticism say that one should not be reading books, for true enlightenment cannot be found in them. Anyway, Lings, who had been initiated into the 'Alawi order in 1938, had set up his own group of Sufis in London.

Harvey wrote to Lings, who suggested that they meet at the British Museum. Then Lings invited him to join his group, which met in a house in the south of England. There about a dozen people used to change into Arab robes before praying, reciting the name of God and drinking mint tea. Lings also used to give out homilies and would occasionally read out letters from his master, Schuon. In Lings's own house in London, he and his wife lived as Arabs, with Arab clothes, furnishings and food. For a while Harvey studied esotericism with him, but he found Lings's version of Sufism too intellectual and lacking in intensity and, besides, Harvey was getting bored with trekking down to Surrey. (I was to meet Lings only once, in circumstances that I will relate later.) Harvey decided to go the source, which was Mostaganem, a small town in western Algeria.

Mostaganem was where Shaikh Ahmad ibn Mustafa al-'Alawi (1869–1934) had founded a new *tariqa*, the 'Alawiya, that was a breakaway from the Darqawi *tariqa*, which had in turn broken away from the Shadhili *tariqa*, and, through this chain of initiatic transmission, the 'Alawiya could trace their *silsila*, or spiritual lineage, all the way back to 'Ali and the Prophet Muhammad. Al-'Alawi had established a *zawiya* in Mostaganem. A *zawiya* is a kind of monastery, except that there is no expectation that its inhabitants should spend the rest of their lives there and celibacy is downright disapproved of. It was a place of retreat, but not a permanent one. The *faqir* should go into the world and find work. Al-'Alawi had started out doing things like fire-walking and snake-charming, but, as he progressed, he became more spiritual, for he came to realise that the important thing was to charm the soul. The 'Alawi *tariqa* was established in 1911. He used spiritual retreats, recitations of the name of God and a dervish dance to bring his disciples to a state of enlightenment. He published poetry and spiritual treatises. Since he was one of the few Sufi masters in Algeria to speak good French, he was often visited by Europeans, many of whom reported that he seemed to be a Christ-like figure. However, he was not popular with the French authorities, as he urged the Algerians to be mindful of their identity and their culture. The order he presided over was strictly orthodox and traditionalist and it had branches all over the Middle East and Europe. (There were 'Alawi *zawiya*s for Arab sailors in Cardiff and Newcastle.) By the time he died he had almost 200,000 disciples.

Harvey had travelled out with Anne. She was at least as remarkable as Harvey. Australian in origin, she was a musician and had played with orchestras in Australia. She had studied Serbo-Croatian in Croatia. She also was a judo black belt and a brilliant linguist. I still have her Croatian grammar and Sanskrit dictionary. In Oxford she lived in a tiny garret for which she paid ten shillings a week. She had met Harvey at a meeting of the Buddhist Society. She was studying Sanskrit and Pali with Robin Zaehner, the Spalding Professor of Eastern Religions and Ethics at All Souls. Zaehner, who was shocked by Anne's bohemian ways, asked rhetorically, 'Did she never wash? Or did she take baths and then cake the dirt on afterwards?' He also compared her to the eighteenth-century traveller and eccentric Lady Hester Stanhope. Anne was indeed tough and adventurous and when a Moroccan military commander in the Sahara had tried to rape her, she had stabbed him in the balls.

From Harvey and Anne, in talks that inevitably went on till we heard the dawn chorus, I learned about the *Zawiya* 'Alawiya in Mostaganem, a place where God made his presence powerfully felt and where ecstasies and miracles were daily occurrences. They had been there and experienced these things. Both had tried at first to resist the pull of the *zawiya*. Lings had previously told Harvey that the Sufis of Mostaganem were members of a degenerate *tariqa* and that, though there were some good things there, the chain of transmission had become hereditary and their spiritual practice routinised. As for Anne, she was steeped in Hinduism and Buddhism and she was at first reluctant to follow the devotional way of Sufism.

Harvey had been initiated as a Sufi by Shaikh Hadj Mehdi Bentounes. Shaikh al-'Alawi had died in 1934 and had been succeeded as Shaikh of the order by Hadj Adda Bentounes and when Hadj Adda died in 1952 then Hadj Mehdi Bentounes became Shaikh. During Harvey's first visit to Mostaganem he had begged to be initiated, but the power of the place had so worked upon him that the Shaikh judged him to be not in his right mind and told him that he could only be initiated once he had cooled down and returned to something like normality. A few months later a group of disciples in a car arrived in Oxford and collected Harvey and took him to the 'Alawi *Zawiya* in Paris at Ivry-sur-Seine, where the Shaikh gave him the initiation. Subsequently Harvey visited Lings just once more and Lings told him that he could see that he had experienced *hal* (ecstasy) and that he was happy for him.

At first sight the embrace of Islam hardly seemed to be the yellow-brick road to personal fulfilment. It was not the religion of choice for hippies in search of exotic spirituality, most of whom opted for some variety of Hinduism or Buddhism, and consequently the hippy trail led through Iran and Afghanistan to India. The overseas empire of psychedelia included Tangier, Marrakesh, Formentera and Kathmandu, but not Mostaganem. It is hard to think back to the sixties in Britain, to a time before Islam had become closely associated with terrorism, a time before Muslims demanded the protection of the law against blasphemies against the Prophet and sought the imposition of Shari'a law in Britain. Prior to the Rushdie affair and the burning of *The Satanic Verses* in 1988, British Muslims hardly ever featured in the newspapers and Islamic fundamentalism was not a topic of interest. In the Middle East and North Africa, the future seemed to belong to the secularists and socialists, such as Egypt's Colonel Nasser, Tunisia's Habib Bourguiba and the Algerian FLN. Surely Islam would slowly and quietly wither away, in the way that Christianity was obviously doing, in a century that would continue to be dominated by rationalism, secularism and liberalism?

But Harvey and Anne spoke of a highly spiritual form of Islam and a version of Sufism that was not drawn from books and which had an unbookish urgency. According to Harvey's guru, Abdullah Faid (who was to become my guru too), 'We are now in a prophetic time. The world is in the same state as before a prophet comes, but since no prophet will come, it is necessary to stay strongly attached to the *tariqa*. For without it even a saint is lost, since now is the time of the Antichrist. The *tariqa* is firmly attached to God, but it remains an island submerged in a sea of irreligion. One must be firmly attached to the *tariqa* without seeking to understand, or question or judge. One must be patient and accept.' The *zawiya* was continually under siege from fifty devils. The spirit of Dajjal (the Muslim Antichrist) was rife and the coming of the Mahdi was imminent.

Then abruptly Anne was no longer with us. She had fled Oxford and headed back to Algeria. On the way, she had called in on the 'Alawi's Paris *zawiya* and its *fuqara* gave her money for the train to Marseilles. (*Fuqara* is the Arabic broken plural of *faqir* – don't ask.) Once in Mostaganem she converted to Islam and was initiated into the 'Alawi *tariqa*. Harvey's initiation had simply involved his taking the hand of the Shaikh, whereas Anne, being female, had to drink from a glass of water into which the Shaikh had dipped two of his fingers. At the moment she drank it a great cloud lifted from her. She was given the name Taqiyya. She was spending all her time before the tombs of the Shaikhs, where she would recite a *dhikr*. (*Dhikr* means the incessant repetition of certain words or formulas in praise of God.) But the next thing we heard she was dead. She had gone to the hammam in preparation for some religious ceremony and caught pneumonia, as a consequence of the sharp differences in temperature inside and outside the hammam. As the pneumonia had worsened, the Shaikh had offered to fly her to America for treatment, but she had refused. The *fuqara* had regarded her as a kind of saint and in the years to come I was to hear a great deal about her last days. On the day of her funeral the imam who regularly presided over the funerals could not be present, so the Shaikh led the prayers, the first time that he had done that for anyone. Bees were said to have prayed at her graveside. They had lined up in straight rows just as Muslims do. Eventually her parents arrived in Algeria to take her body back to Australia. It was reported that when her body was disinterred it smelt of honey. Harvey took her death very hard and he spent many days staring at the wall and hardly speaking at all.

Besides having listened to Harvey and Anne, I had learned some more about Sufism in a conventional fashion – by attending the lectures of Zaehner. These took place in his rooms in All Souls. There was no need for a larger lecture hall since I was his entire audience that spring term. He sat in one armchair and I in another. Within minutes of first encountering him, it became apparent that he was steeped in French literature and in his opening remarks he made reference to Proust and Bernanos. But to me Zaehner was just another of my teachers and it was a while before I understood what an interesting man he was. At the age of twenty he had experienced a sort of mystical ecstasy while reading Rimbaud's 'Ô saisons, ô châteaux' and this had led him on to the study of Oriental mysticism. He also became a devout Roman Catholic (and yet he apparently believed that Muhammad was a true prophet).

Apart from French, he had mastered Sanskrit, Arabic, Latin, Greek, Albanian, Persian, Avestan and Pali, as well as the useful European languages. He had returned from a visit to Iran a few days before term started and, when another All Souls don looked in on him, Zaehner described how terrified he had been when the plane he was on had been pursued by fireballs, as if some malign spirit had it in for him. Bespectacled, prone to giggling and by then in his fifties, he gave the appearance of being a timid man, but he cannot have been so very timid. During the war he had been an intelligence officer in Iran, working a lot with the hill tribes in the north with the task of thwarting German attempts at sabotaging the railway that carried Allied supplies through Iran to the Soviet Union. (He spoke cryptically of having done terrible things during the war.) After the war he returned to Iran in 1951 and played a leading part in organising the thugs whose street riots forced Mossadegh to resign as Prime Minister in 1953 and so brought the Anglo-Iranian Oil Company under British control once more. At some point after the war, he had been denounced as a pro-Soviet spy by a Russian defector, though an investigation had found him to be not guilty. However, he had certainly associated with Philby and Burgess. In 1952, having become the Spalding Professor of Eastern Religions and Ethics, he gave a notorious inaugural lecture, for though the Spalding Professorship was supposed to have the purpose of bringing 'the great religious systems … together in closer understanding, harmony and friendship', he denounced this notion as erroneous and heretical. He believed that the alleged transcendent unity of the great faiths was a piece of dangerous nonsense, based on careless analogies and identifications of very different types of religious experiences and dogmas, and he was scornful of the notion of the mystical unity of all religions. (Quite different from Schuon, then.)

He taught me a lot about Sufi doctrine, or at least he tried to. I still have my lecture notes, but they are horribly confused. One of the minor problems was that I had no idea how to spell Arabic names. It was more of a problem that I had a disorderly mind. I collected enigmatic quotations and instances of weird happenings, but remained oblivious to the structure and direction of Zaehner's arguments. Vaguely occult doodles ran down the pages of my notes. From my notes, I see that I learned that Avicenna regarded belief in the resurrection a tiresome distraction; that Ibn Tufayl cast a treatise on natural theology in the form of romance about a boy who grew up alone on a desert island and who had to discover everything for himself, including the existence of God; that, according to al-Junayd, Iblis (the Devil) was shocked by the sin of Adam; that, also according to al-Junayd, 'Intoxication is the playground of the children and sobriety the field of death for good men'; that Jesus in Islam taught that 'The world is like a bridge. Therefore pass over it lightly'; and, according to Abu Yazid al-Bistami, 'The man who advances along the mystic path is lashed with the whip of love, pierced by the sword of longing and propped up against the gates of All.'

Though Zaehner's lectures were certainly scholarly, they nevertheless evinced quite a lot of prejudice against certain aspects of Sufism. He pointed to the arrogance of ascetics. He argued that, in seeking union with God, a misguided mystic might come under the delusion that he actually was God. The ninth-century Persian Sufi Abu Yazid al-Bistami was a case in point, for he proclaimed, 'Glory be to me! How great is my glory!' According to Zaehner, Abu Yazid was a manic depressive. He speculated that al-Junayd might have been a manic depressive too. Zaehner accused Sufis of having a Manichaean dislike of women. He also talked cryptically about the Sufi dream world or game world. Towards the end of the day a strong gin and tonic would be served – more gin than tonic. In his quiet, comfortable study he spoke gravely about placing oneself in the hands of a Sufi shaikh like a corpse on the slab in the hands of the undertaker, as well as self-mortification, delirious ecstasy, personal extinction before God and the willing embrace of hellfire. But Zaehner was lecturing from books. He was looking at Sufism from the outside. There is little or no sense of mysticism as lived experience in his lectures or writings (though I am quite sure that he knew what that was like). As the Sufi Abu Said ibn Abi'l-Khayr observed, 'The first step in this affair is the breaking of ink pots and the tearing up of books and the forgetting of all kinds of knowledge.' One day I told Zaehner that I had to be in London at the time of next week's lecture. He looked at me sadly: 'I think that we might bring this course of lectures to an end now, don't you?'

However, I was to re-encounter Zaehner in my third year and in the meantime I devoured his book *Mysticism, Sacred and Profane: An Inquiry into Some Varieties of Praeternatural Experience* (1957) for what it could tell me about mescaline. In mid-sixties Britain there was very little drugs literature readily available. There was Aldous Huxley's rapturous account of what he judged to be a genuine religious experience on mescaline. This was written up in a long essay, 'The Doors of Perception' (1954), and republished by Penguin together with another essay, 'The Doors of Heaven and Hell'. In his youth Huxley had written some rather good satirical novels, but later in life he turned to a woolly, Californian form of Hinduism. He was convinced that by taking mescaline he had passed through a 'Door in the Wall' into a form of high mystical experience and 'the man who comes back through the Door in the Wall will never be quite the same as the man who went out. He will be wiser but less sure, happier but less self-satisfied, humbler in acknowledging his ignorance yet better equipped to understand the relationship of words to things, of systematic reasoning to the unfathomable mystery which it tries, forever vainly, to comprehend.' (Obviously, this is Huxley boasting about how humble he is while at the same time revealing that he is an enlightened being.)

Zaehner's *Mysticism, Sacred and Profane* contained an onslaught on Huxley's muddled and vainglorious presentation of his trips as spiritual experiences. Zaehner denounced the godless and woolly doctrine that 'all is one' and instead he exalted God-based mystical experience within the context of an established religion. In an appendix, he described his own experience with mescaline, which he had taken under medical supervision in his room at All Souls. Though it was obviously quite a giggly experience, his conclusion was downbeat: 'I would not presume to draw any conclusions from so trivial an experience. It was interesting and it was hilariously funny. All along, however, I felt that the experience was in a sense "anti-religious", I mean, not conformable with religious experience or in the same category.' So Huxley was deluding himself. Mescaline could not produce the 'natural mystical experience'. Zaehner concluded, 'Finally, the fact that I am an assiduous reader of *Alice Through the Looking-Glass* is probably not irrelevant to the nature of my experience.' As he saw it, Huxley had no previous religious experience to draw on and his '"conversion" to a Vedāntin way of life was due to little more than a total rejection of everything that modern civilization stands for and to a deep-seated aversion to historical Christianity …'

I devoured both Huxley's and Zaehner's books indiscriminately, not really terribly aware that they were saying quite different things. When I took LSD, a drug that is pretty similar to mescaline, my experience of it fell somewhere between Huxley's awed sense of entering a territory previously inhabited only by William Blake and a handful of Indian mystics and Zaehner's high-spirited irreverence. I took LSD when it was still legal and the ampoules I broke open and poured into orange juice came from a Sandoz laboratory where LSD was being tested to see if it affected muscle flexibility in animals. (Scientists, eh?) I remember the elephant-headed Hindu god Ganesha sitting on my ceiling and handing me down a cigarette. Despite the frequent appearance of Hindu gods in my visions, these trips did not feel like religious experiences – still less so when the ghosts of scantily clothed women rose like brightly coloured smoke from the pages of *Playboy*.

In *Brideshead Revisited* Evelyn Waugh had written of Oxford in the following terms: 'her autumnal mists, her grey springtime, and the rare glory of her summer days … when the chestnut was in flower and the bells rang out high and clear over her gables and cupolas, exhaled the soft airs of centuries of youth. It was this cloistral hush which gave our laughter its resonance, and carried it still joyously, over the intervening clamour.' The effect of all these sorts of thing was enhanced when one was on LSD.

Drug-taking for me was not recreational. In those days few people, if any, took drugs to go clubbing. Taking a drug might be a step towards understanding the Meaning of Life, or a portal into a world that was out of the ordinary, and it was also a kind of rite of passage. When I was on a trip I always had a notebook to hand and I brought back a lot of scribbled garbage as messages from the other world. For me, taking a drug usually started off pretty earnestly, even if I often ended up laughing. Of course, drug-taking strengthened the conviction that the world was not what it seemed and that it did indeed come equipped with escape hatches. 'I was at Oxford from 1964 to 1968,' recalls Julian Barnes, the novelist. 'I wore my hair long and had a pair of purple jeans which were excruciatingly uncomfortable, but I knew only one person who ever mentioned drugs.'

Evidently I was at the other Oxford, for I knew hardly anyone who was not on drugs. Howard Marks was the leading dealer in Oxford then and some of the stuff I took came ultimately from him. I believe that in the long run, in the years that followed, my consumption of dangerous drugs, including LSD, cocaine, heroin, opium, amyl nitrite and Methedrine, helped cure my craziness, for they gave me a perspective on life as well as a social circle and the currency of conversation. They also assuaged the devastating boredom from which I suffered so much of the time. But when I asked myself whether drugs could provide a pathway to enlightenment, it was plain to me that they were a dead end. I would have to go to Mostaganem.

4. King Solomon and his army of jinn

3

ALGERIA

ON 8 MAY 1945 a demonstration in favour of Algerian independence in the small town of Sétif turned violent and
attempts by the French authorities to control the march
provoked the Muslims to turn on the European colonists in
the region. Farmers were attacked by their servants. Villages
were looted and set on fire. One hundred and three Europeans were murdered. Some of the men had their penises cut
off and stuffed in their mouths, and some of the women,
many of whom were first the victims of rape, had their
breasts cut off. The French army when it arrived savagely
repressed the uprising and made use of summary executions and indiscriminate bombardments to do so. Vigilante
groups of European settlers went out on lynch hunts for
Muslims and killed at least 6,000.

At that time Algeria was part of metropolitan France.
It was not regarded by the government as a colony and all
the Europeans who lived in Algeria could vote in France's
national elections. But only a tiny minority of the Muslims,
who constituted nine-tenths of the country's population,
had full citizenship and voting rights. Although the fero-
cious way the Sétif revolt had been crushed inaugurated a
period of uneasy peace, the insurrection broke out anew
in 1954. This time the revolt was more widespread and

prolonged. It ushered in a war of unparalleled brutality. The FLN (Front de Libération National) made expert use of guerrilla attacks and atrocity. The French army responded with mass reprisals and the regular use of torture in order to break up terrorist cells. They also recruited many thousands of Arabs and Berbers into their ranks. These troops were known as *harkis*.

Alastair Horne's *A Savage War of Peace* is a masterpiece of military history; its tense narration mingles politics and strategy with accounts of horrific bloodletting and mass sadism. When it was published in 1977, I bought a copy and stayed awake till five in the morning to finish reading it. I have no wish to follow Horne in chronicling the horrors of this war. But it is important to be aware just how savage the 'Savage War' was. As an example, only one atrocity will be related here, the massacre of the Europeans by their Muslim neighbours in the small mining hamlet of El-Halia in 1955. The French paras reached the place too late. In Horne's words:

> An appalling sight greeted them. In houses literally awash with blood, European mothers were found with their throats slit and their bellies slashed open by bill-hooks. Children had suffered the same fate, and infants in arms had their brains dashed out against the wall. Four families had been wiped out down to the last member; only six who had barricaded themselves in a house in the centre of the village and had held out with sporting rifles and revolvers had escaped unscathed. Men returning home from the mine had been ambushed in their cars and hacked to pieces. Altogether thirty-seven Europeans had died, including ten children under fifteen; another thirteen had been left for dead.

When the paras found Arab boys kicking in an old woman's severed head in the street they shot them dead instantly and they went on to take reprisals on a spectacular scale, so that they had to use bulldozers to bury the Arabs they had machine-gunned. Elsewhere gangs of *pieds noirs* (French colonialists resident in Algeria) roamed the countryside looking for Arabs to kill. Thousands died. When, many years later, I started to research my novel *The Mysteries of Algiers*, I came across a booklet put out by the French army at the time. It was full of photographs of victims of the FLN, including those men whose penises had been hacked off and shoved in their mouths before their heads were severed. Algeria was a cruel country then and it still is.

The struggle to root out the terrorist network in the Algiers Kasbah has been brilliantly recreated in Gillo Pontecorvo's remarkable feature film *The Battle of Algiers* (1966), perhaps the most powerful political film ever made. It showed the ruthlessness of both sides, as the Algerians used terrorism and the French used torture and both sides used murder. Although it is remarkably even-handed in its coverage of what went on in Algiers in the late fifties, some have taken the film to be propaganda for armed struggle against colonialism. As the film shows, torture proved to be effective and French soldiers became expert at it. They used water pumps to fill the bellies of Algerians and they attached electrodes to their penises. The case of Djamila Boupacha, who was deflowered with the neck of a bottle and tortured with lighted cigarette ends, as well as having electrodes attached to her nipples and her vagina, caused particular scandal among Left Bank intellectuals in France, though the *pieds noirs* warmly supported what the army was doing and most French citizens preferred not to know what was going on. Subsequently I met a *faqir* who, after he had been tortured by the French, had had salt rubbed in his wounds.

The books of the Martiniquais doctor Franz Fanon, like those of Hermann Hesse and R. D. Laing, were favoured student reading in the sixties. Fanon's writings were on the serious edge of the counterculture. He had worked as a psychiatrist in a hospital in Blida, a little south of Algiers, and had seen terrible things, most of which he judged to be the product of the degradation that came from being colonised. In writings like *Les Damnés de la terre* (translated into English as *The Wretched of the Earth*), he preached the cathartic value of violence. Only violence could cleanse the colonised people of the shame of having been under white man's rule. Colonialism was a form of violence and it could only be resisted by violence: 'Violence alone, violence committed by the people, violence organised and educated by its leaders, makes it possible for the masses to understand social truths and gives the key to them.' Only through murder and spectacular cruelty could that inferiority complex be cured. Violence was not an option, but a necessity: 'The naked truth of decolonisation evokes for us the searing bullets and bloodstained knives which emanate from it.' Though a boulevard and a university in Algeria are named after him, his bloodthirsty visionary rhetoric has turned out to be a cursed legacy to his adopted country.

The French army won the Battle of the Kasbah, just as they were winning the war in the desert, but they were still losing the political war. The FLN was supported by all the Arab countries, whereas France had little or no support from the United States or Europe. The army was already demoralised by its previous withdrawal from Vietnam. French citizens on the mainland wearied of the demands made upon them by the *pieds noirs*. In June 1958 General de Gaulle arrived in Algiers and made the famous speech in which he told the assembled thousands, '*Je vous ai compris.*' Subsequently, he toured other Algerian towns, including Mostaganem, where a vast crowd greeted his '*Vive l'Algérie française! Vive la République!*' with wild enthusiasm. The 'Alawi *tariqa* in Mostaganem supported the Algerian uprising and later there were protests when seven Arab citizens

5. General de Gaulle addressing the *pieds noirs* of Mostaganem. They understood him to be promising them that Algeria would remain French

of Mostaganem died under torture. French soldiers fired on and killed demonstrators in the town. Khaled Bentounes, the son of my future Shaikh, remembers that the man who helped him and other children escape was himself shot down. When De Gaulle visited Mostaganem in 1958 he had a meeting with the Shaikh. Later, I heard from the *fuqara* that the *Zawiya* in Mostaganem had sheltered the principal leader of the fight for liberation, Ben Bella, when he was on the run and hence, after liberation, when other *tariqa*s were being shut down, the *Zawiya* was tolerated – though only just – but this is not a story that I have been able to confirm.

In the last days of French rule in 1961 the OAS (Organisation de l'Armée Secrète) launched a final scorched-earth campaign in which oil installations, the University of Algiers and much else were destroyed.

The OAS's tactics only made it more inevitable that most *pieds noirs* would have to get out with whatever they could carry with them. By August 1962 nearly a million of them had left. A small minority, who believed in the guarantees offered to them by the new regime, stayed, but many were then abducted and 'disappeared'. Those that were still alive had their property confiscated and eventually they too left. As they left, the delightful beaches became deserted, bars and patisseries closed and churches were boarded up. The FLN moved in to the big cities and set about slaughtering the *harkis*. An estimated 70,000 *harkis* were tortured and killed, many of them by being buried alive.

Still, independence was achieved in 1962 and for most Algerians it delusively promised days of hope. Khaled, then thirteen and the adopted son of Shaikh Hadj Adda, remembers carrying the Algerian flag through Mostaganem in the celebration. Cakes and Coca-Cola were distributed. Ahmed Ben Bella, the new head of state, was handsome and charismatic. He announced that democracy was a luxury that Algeria could not afford and he had some of his political opponents murdered or driven into exile. He had grand plans, many of them on an international scale, but he was really the army's figurehead and eventually the army wearied of him and his grand plans and in a smartly executed coup deposed him. On 19 June 1965 troops acting on the dour and taciturn Houari Boumedienne's orders arrested Ben Bella. Pontecorvo's *Battle of Algiers* was being filmed in the Kasbah at the time and many people thought that the troops they saw moving around the city were Pontecorvo's actors. No one was sure what was happening. There were tanks in the streets of Algiers that summer and it was at this point I had decided that I had to go to Algeria in search of spiritual enlightenment.

It was still dark when I left the Surrey village of Chobham, heading successively for Woking, Waterloo and Fenchurch

6. A still from Gillo Pontecorvo's *The Battle of Algiers*, released in 1966, showing 'Colonel Mathieu' marching in front of his paras. 'Mathieu', who authorised the use of torture in order to secure an apparent victory in the Battle of Algiers Kasbah in 1957, was a composite figure based on several real-life French officers, notably Brigadier General Jacques Massu

Street. In my rucksack I carried a copy of Martin Lings's *A Moslem Saint of the Twentieth Century*, A. J. Arberry's translation of the Qur'an, a paperback of James Elroy Flecker's *Hassan*, Johan Huizinga's *The Waning of the Middle Ages*, a tin full of medicines, a wad of traveller's cheques and five pounds' worth of French money, a compass, a sheath knife, a map of France, a sleeping bag, toilet paper and an empty notebook. Most of the passengers on the ferry from Tilbury crowded into its casino. Paris was beautiful, but I had to keep moving. On the way down through France I slept on the floor of someone else's hotel room, in a station waiting room, under a motorway bridge and in a youth hostel.

When I reached Marseilles it took several days wandering around the industrial harbour in order to find a boat that was sailing to Algeria and in the meantime I spent the balmy nights sleeping on a beach outside the city. Finally, I found a boat belonging to the Compagnie Transatlantique et Mixte that would take me to Algiers (but not to Oran, as I had hoped).

Before boarding the boat, I bought a loaf of bread, also two posters of Françoise Hardy which I mailed home. So I then had no French money and just the loaf and it turned out that this and an apple and a bag of peanuts had to last me thirty-six hours. Since I was travelling fourth class, I was in a long queue composed mostly of Algerians – the first time I had ever met any. I thought them rather good-looking and strikingly good-natured. But once I had boarded the boat, I was directed to a special part of a deck reserved for fourth-class, poor whites (and one Algerian who had a French wife). It was crowded and God knows what the Algerian deck was like. I sat in the lotus posture and contemplated the Christ-like photograph of al-'Alawi in Lings's book. As the day progressed, the heat built up agreeably. It can never be too hot for me. At night there was barely space to stretch out to sleep.

By night the lights of Algiers, spreading across the hills above the harbour bay, promised a place of enchantment. It took three and a half hours to pass through customs. The whites, most of whom had travelled first or second class, were now firmly placed at the back of the long queue that trailed along the length of the quay. Large white cockroaches were the first living creatures I encountered when I set foot in Africa. It was dark when I entered the city and the streets were crawling with soldiers and armed police. Having cashed a traveller's cheque for Algerian dinars, I entered a restaurant and ordered a great bowl of couscous, but my stomach had shrunk so much that I could only eat a few mouthfuls. The following morning I cleaned my teeth for the first time in days before walking out into the heat and the blinding white light. Algiers was as magnificent by day as by night. The Kasbah, the close-packed, maze-like Arab quarter, was high up on the hill. In what had been the European sector of the city, the boulevards, flanked by grand white buildings with blue shutters and awnings, plunged down to the edge of the brilliant sea.

At last I was on an adventure! For my generation, hitch-hiking was a youthful rite of passage, just as the Grand Tour had been for the young men of the eighteenth century. I hitchhiked along the coast road, a landscape of Roman ruins among the cacti and cork and fig trees under a brilliant sky. It was mostly lorries on the road, though the occasional smart car driven by a Frenchman passed me. There were also a lot of goats on the road. Those Algerian lorry drivers who gave me lifts usually talked about the horrors of the war and the atrocities committed by the French; the French who gave me lifts talked about Arab atrocities. I drank at village pumps, I bought melons at eight dinars each and bread and stole grapes from the edges of those vineyards which were unguarded, but some of the vineyards had sentries with guns and they would watch and spit as I passed by (Algerians are marvellous spitters). Sentries apart, there were almost always people sitting on the edge of the road doing nothing. Silent men at the doors of huts of mud and straw gazed out at me.

The run-down hotel in Gouraya had a wooden fridge and no running water. I went to sleep in my sleeping bag, so as not to have to rest on the filthy sheet, but I was awoken a little after midnight to find a double-barrelled shotgun pointing at my face. The enraged owner, who had just returned from hunting, wanted to know what I was doing sleeping in his hotel. The boy who had shown me to my room had not stayed to tell the hotelier that he had a paying guest. Outside Ténès I slept in a cave that had been a Phoenician tomb overlooking the sea. It was reached by a narrow ledge. By the dying light of the sun I read the ghost and caravan episodes from Flecker's *Hassan*. The latter contained lines that I memorised as I travelled:

We are the Pilgrims, master; we shall go
Always a little further: it may be
Beyond that last blue mountain barred with snow
Across the angry or that glimmering sea,
White on a throne or guarded in a cave
There lies a prophet who can understand
Why men were born; but surely we are brave,
Who take the Golden Road to Samarkand.

And a little further down the page:

We travel not for trafficking alone:
By hotter winds our fiery hearts are fanned:
For lust of knowing what should not be known,
We take the road to Samarkand.

As I sat in the cave-tomb listening to the beating waves and the call of the nightjar, I had a feeling that is hard to describe, but which was perhaps a sense that I was about to engage with destiny. This sensation has recurred only a handful of times in my life.

The following morning a lorry driver gave me a lift and, when I told him where I was going, he said that he had given lifts before to Germans and English and always they were going to Mostaganem. Why Mostaganem?

It took about four days of buses and lifts before I reached that town. I own a copy of the *Guide Bleu* for Algeria dating from 1955 (so printed a year after the fatal insurrection had broken out). According to the *Guide*, Mostaganem's population was then 53,000. Really the place was two towns, for the Europeans had dominated Mostaganem proper, while the Arabs were tightly packed in the native part, which was called Tijdit. Metaphorically and literally the two towns were separated by a chasm created by the flow of the 'Ayn Sefra (the Yellow Spring) down to the sea. The European half had two hotels, a big square, a park and a grand Avenue Anatole France. It was a perfectly formed small French town with a fishing port. As for the native quarter, the *Guide Bleu* noted almost nothing of interest there, except for the *Zawiya* of Shaikh Ahmed al-'Alawi, who, it reported, was the head of a Sufi order numbering over 100,000 adherents, of whom half were in the Berber Kabyle region. There was an annual gathering of these Sufis every August.

I made my way to the main square of what had been the French town and bought a kilo of grapes, which I started eating immediately. An Arab, passing by, pointed out that I should have washed them first, but I was always careless about things like that. Then some *pieds noirs* sitting at a table outside the Café Oriental called me over. The café's delighted patron treated me to two large cups of coffee. He and his French and Italian clientele were so pleased to see a new white face in town. I was mistaken for the herald of British tourism. Maybe things would turn out all right for these *pieds noirs* who had chosen to hang on in what was really their town? (But when I returned the following year all but one or two of them were gone.)

I did not linger long in Mostaganem proper. A bus took me into Tijdit and a crowd of friendly locals led me to the door of the *Zawiya*. (I was lucky in the people I met that day. Many of the Mostaganese hated the *Zawiya* and consequently would deny all knowledge of its whereabouts.)

Anyway, I was led through the mosque of the new part of the *Zawiya* into the courtyard. A crowd of curious *fuqara*

7. Tijdit, the Arab quarter of Mostaganem

clustered round me. I fished about in my rucksack and brought out my copy of Lings's book about al-'Alawi. The *fuqara* gazed with reverence at the frontispiece photo of Shaikh al-'Alawi. Before I left, I donated the book to the *Zawiya* and later I learned that it had been taken to Oran to be translated into French.

The minute I stepped into the *Zawiya* I had begun to feel a little strange, as if slightly drunk. Slightly 'drunk', hungry and travel-stained, I was entrusted to a man wearing a white skullcap with the beginnings of a yellow turban wrapped around it, which served to conceal his baldness. Abdullah Faid had a red beard, though the red was the creation of henna, and the beard also showed streaks of grey. He had an ingenuous, childlike face (but Ralph Davis at Merton had taught me to be wary of seemingly childlike intelligences). Faid's slightly bulging eyes were troubled. His muscular arms were those of the sailor he once had been. I took him to be a Frenchman, but he swiftly corrected this misconception. He was a Breton. The name he had been christened with was Joseph Gabriel Le Mer. He made coffee and, since he never went in for small talk, he started to speak straight

54

away about the interior life and the way of the heart. At this point I should say that I owed my mystical instruction in Mostaganem to a C pass in O-level French, plus some remedial teaching in Oxford, and it is certainly possible that I misunderstood some things.

He talked without ceasing or thinking. It was as if he was motorised. He told me that I must always follow the heart. The Shaikh al-'Alawi once said to his *fuqara*, 'If I told you the truth, you would drive me out of this *zawiya*.' According to Faid, 'Taqiyya [Anne] is not dead. She is with the spirits that guide us.' One day in Casablanca, Faid was very hot (both spiritually and physically) and he prayed in front of an inscription of the Divine Name, Allah. As he prayed, water came flowing out of the Name and he drank it. Even animals, birds and insects in the *Zawiya* were *fuqara*. One had to be respectful to the flies that infested the place, for they would talk to you with the voice of the Shaikh.

Faid had been in the *Zawiya* twenty-two years or more. The first time he witnessed the *'imara*, the sacred Sufi dance (literally 'plenitude'), in England he had fallen into a faint. One of the other *fuqara*, 'Umar the builder, had described Faid as always hot ('*chaud*'). 'That is very good,' he had added. Mostaganem is the crossroads of all religions – the place where their transcendent unity is made apparent. When the Shaikh al-'Alawi used to go into town to the great mosque, people trembled when they saw him. So great was his spirit. One needs the Shaikh's guidance to practise the *Ism al-Azm* (the Great Name), or else one is lost. Do not seek to penetrate the mystery of God. If there were no mysteries in the *tariqa*, there would be no God. The present Shaikh suffers. He is always ill. The Shaikh al-'Alawi was the same. They both take upon themselves the evil of other people. One day a man and his wife prayed, saying, 'The Shaikh suffers so much. Let us take upon ourselves a little of his suffering.' And God granted them this and it drove them insane. Their suffering was horrible, fantastic in its power. Eventually the woman killed her husband while he slept. The Shaikh al-'Alawi was almost pure spirit. His body was very thin. He hardly ate. When he held his hand up to the light, you could see through it to the bones.

Since there were many difficult people in the *Zawiya*, it was a place of trials. Madness was a danger here. One 'Alawi disciple, after prolonged meditation, returned to earth announcing not that he was the one God, as the medieval Sufi al-Hallaj had done, but two equal and omnipotent Gods. It took the *fuqara* a long time to draw him out of his insanity. I was fascinated. (I was familiar with madness. My father was Superintendent of Holloway Sanatorium and, before that, a consultant psychiatrist there. As a schoolboy, I regularly read the *Lancet* and the *British Journal of Psychiatry*. When I was younger one of the annual ordeals was an event which my brother and I christened the Lunatics' Christmas Ball.)

The previous Shaikh, Shaikh Hadj Adda, once said, 'If we had not known that there were only three prophets, I should have said that Abdullah Faid was one.' But Faid was a *majdhub*, a holy fool, someone crazed by God. *Majdhub* literally means 'attracted' and so it can be taken to refer to someone who has been drawn to God and then not fully returned to earth.

In *Manners and Customs of the Modern Egyptians*, first published in 1836, Edward William Lane wrote of the *majdhub* as being regarded by the Egyptians

> as a being whose mind is in heaven, while his grosser part mingles among ordinary mortals; consequently, he is considered an especial favourite of heaven. Whatever enormities a reputed saint may commit (and there are many who are constantly infringing precepts of their religion), such acts do not affect his fame for sanctity; for they are considered as the results of the abstraction of his mind

56

from worldly things; his soul, or reasoning faculties, being wholly absorbed in devotion; so that his passions are left without control.

(But here I should observe that Faid did not infringe the precepts of his religion.) The great French Orientalist Louis Massignon once described *majdhub*s as 'court fools in the service of the wider public of the believers'. According to another Orientalist, Émile Dermenghem, 'They have no break on their impulses; they give voice to profound truths, presented in paradoxical formations.'

Faid was quite open about his status as a *majdhub* and he regarded Sidi Ahmed (Harvey) as, like himself, a *majdhub*. Harvey had been and gone. I had missed him by a few days. Faid raved on about how Harvey had passed into ecstasy a week ago: 'He contemplated, he wept and he opened his heart to love. He is really mystic.' Faid thought that Harvey, long-haired and white-robed, resembled *Sayyidna Isa* (Our Lord Jesus), though this perception was to change. He talked also about Anne, who had passed away in blissful prayer. Faid had poured water on her grave.

Besides being a *majdhub*, Faid was also a *mujarred*. A *mujarred* is a *faqir* who renounces worldly pursuits in order to reside in the *Zawiya* at the disposition of the Shaikh. But only a few people were allowed to do this in Mostaganem and most of the Shaikh's followers were instructed to go out into the world and work and marry.

After coffee, Faid led me to one of the hammams in Tijdit. As I stripped down, a huge towel was wrapped around my waist and I was handed wooden clogs. In the weeks and years that followed I became very familiar with the routines of the hammam. Having stripped, I tied the cloth round my waist to conceal my private parts and then entered the steamy caldarium, where men sat on stools sluicing water over themselves. I sat on a stool and soaped and rinsed myself. The Western idea of a bath, in which one lies in a tub full of dirty water, was regarded by these Muslims as unsanitary. There was a great slab in the centre of the room on which massages were given. After the major ablutions, or *ghusl*, I was swathed completely in towels and led to a row of beds to rest and quietly sweat. One normally visited the hammam at least once a week prior to the Friday noon prayer, for it was at the hammam that the *ghusl* could be most conveniently performed. (*Ghusl* is obligatory for observant Muslims after the emission of semen.) Every other day was a women's day, but Friday was one of the men's days at the hammam.

Later, at the time of *Maghrib*, the sunset prayer, I was taken into the mosque of the *Zawiya* and I sat at the back to watch the *fuqara* at prayer. Dinner in an adjacent room sitting on the floor was from a communal bowl of couscous, washed down with water from tin mugs. On the walls of the dining room, which was next to the prayer chamber, were garishly coloured pictures of Mecca and Medina, Noah's Ark and Moses bearing the tablets of the law, a press cutting photo of the Cardiff *Zawiya*, two identical photos of the *Zawiya* in Mostaganem and three calendars from the *Zawiya*'s printing press, one of which had photos of the three Shaikhs posted over it. On Faid's walls were fading photographs of aged disciples, a colourful calendar printed by the 'Alawi press in Mostaganem, a cutting from the *Birmingham Post* featuring the present Shaikh visiting 'Alawi disciples in Birmingham and maps of France and the Middle East. By now my sleeping bag had become like a second skin to me and I slept well in it on the floor of this room. I used *A Moslem Saint of the Twentieth Century* wrapped up in a towel as my pillow. Flies, those honorary *fuqara*, settled on the coffee stains. Faid kept his alarm clock in an otherwise empty goldfish bowl. (He once told me that it was necessary for people of a high spiritual state

8. The courtyard of the Zawiya showing the entrance and minaret

to look eccentric in order to appear more human.)

In the days that followed, I became familiar with the *Zawiya* and its rhythms. Shaikh Hadj Adda was very pleased because it was built on the exact model of Paradise. The *saha*, or courtyard, of the newer part of the *Zawiya*, was entered via the prayer area of the mosque. On the floor of the mosque there were large stones scattered here and there on the mats. They baffled me at first, but it turned out that they were for the use of those who, because of some infirmity, were unable to perform the lesser ablutions (of which more shortly) with water. In such circumstances one could use sand or stone as a kind of substitute ablutions. At night the *saha* had an eerie beauty as the lamps on the colonnades cut the courtyard into lozenges of bright marble and the trees outside seemed to hover over the *Zawiya* like corals in a dark sea. White-robed *fuqara* on their way to prayer passed through the shadows. Descending the stairs into the *saha*, the minaret was on the near left-hand corner and Faid's room was on the far right-hand corner. The *saha* was modelled on one in Medina and each room in the *Zawiya* was named after a prophet. Abdullah Muslim was named after Isa (Jesus) and Faid after Musa (Moses). Directly facing the entrance and beyond the marble fountain in the centre was the Throne of God, a triple-arched raised alcove decorated in red. There were seven steps up to this raised open area. Friday was a day for putting things in order, tidying up and cleaning the *Zawiya*.

The communal lavatories (holes in the ground with tap water to clean oneself up) were to the left of the throne. They were reputedly a dangerous haunt of the jinn, though I was less bothered by this than I was by the absence of lavatory paper. The imam's room was to the right. A room in the other corner from Faid's was for the use of the Jeunesse Allaouia, a Sufi youth movement. There were fourteen arches set into each of the side walls. The rooms that ran along the sides of the courtyard were mostly empty. Their floors were covered with rough matting and they could be used for anything. The *fuqara* slept more or less where they felt like. Often we slept on the roofs, though, since some of the *fuqara* were sleepwalkers, this was somewhat perilous. The lesser ablutions for the prayer were usually performed at the basin of the fountain. The lesser ablutions were obligatory after excretion, heavy sleep or being touched erotically by a woman. (The last never happened to me in Mostaganem.) The major ablutions, obligatory after sex or the shedding of blood, was a complete wash and was best performed at a hammam.

The lesser ablutions, which commenced with the invocation of the name of God, involved a series of ritualised movements. First one washed the hands, then the mouth, then the nostrils, then the face, then the arms up to the elbows, the hair (or the baldness if applicable), then the ears and then the feet, and one finished by reciting the *shahada* (or attestation of faith). I was told by Abdullah Muslim to say, 'A'ud bi'llahi min al-shaytan an-rajim. Bismi'laahi al-rahman al-rahim' (I take refuge from Satan, the one who is stoned. In the name of God the Compassionate the Merciful), before starting the *wudu*. Doves came to drink from the fountain and their cooing made a sound like *huwa*, meaning 'He', which the *fuqara* took to refer to God. As I performed the lesser ablutions at that fountain and listened to the cooing of the doves, I would think of T. S. Eliot's *Ash Wednesday* and the lines:

> But the fountain sprang up and the bird sang down
> Redeem the time, redeem the dream.

I used to wash my clothes in the fountain. While I was in the *Zawiya* I also learned to sew on buttons, a skill I have since forgotten. On one occasion Faid sat down at the fountain, planning to wash, when he saw another *faqir* enter whom he really ought to greet, though he decided that he could not be bothered. But then a bee settled in front of him and started washing its feet in a drop from the fountain. So Faid allowed the bee to perform its ablutions first and he took the bee's intervention as a sign that he should after all rise and greet the *faqir* who had just entered.

The old mosque was directly across the road. It was entered via a small courtyard with a fountain and then a vestibule. The prayer room of the old mosque was where the *'imara*, the sacred dance, was usually held. 'Umar Labique's room was to one side and this was where we hunched over communal bowls for lunch and dinner. The library was next door and this led on to the tombs of Shaikh al-'Alawi and Shaikh Hadj Adda. The tomb chamber was dark and thickly carpeted and the air heavy with incense. Sometimes a *faqir* would choose to sleep beside the tombs in the hope of being given a dream of good guidance. (This practice is known in Arabic as *istikhara* and in English as incubation.) Other rooms led off the main prayer area: a schoolroom, a breakfast room and a room where the Shaikh often received visitors. The harem quarters of the Shaikh were next to the old mosque. Until I encountered Selima two years later, I saw nothing of the women in the harem area. So though getting on for a hundred people inhabited the sprawling complex of the *Zawiya*, I never met half of them.

The road between the two mosques ran from the sea up to main square of Tijdit. It was all very peaceful, for there was little traffic. The sky was an important part of the setting of days in the *Zawiya*; it was always a startlingly brilliant blue. From the top of the road the flat-roofed little houses fell away in boxed planes of flaking yellow, spiked with telegraph poles and thick swathes of bulrushes. The track between them was full of broken stones, the rinds of prickly pears and other rotting fruit. There were the remains of sand-walled houses, ruined by flash floods a few decades ago, higher up on the chasm. There was also a wrecked mill and the former home of a Turkish marabout. Whenever I walked along this track, which eventually ran along the edge of the gorge of 'Ayn Sefra, lined with bul-rushes, I would always think of those lines of Coleridge:

> But O, that deep romantic chasm which slanted
> Down the green hill athwart a cedarn cover!
> A savage place! as holy and enchanted
> As e'er beneath a waning moon was haunted
> By woman wailing for her demon-lover!

Humidity gave the light a pearly quality. The sunsets over the sea were customarily spectacularly lurid and prismatic. The bulrushes, the palm trees, the metallic blue sea and the marine sunsets – it was just like living inside an illustrated copy of the Bible.

Time and materiality were twisted about in the *Zawiya*. Once I saw Faid approach at the doorway to his room seconds before he actually entered the courtyard and made his way to that doorway. Not very long after, I saw a small black sparrow-like bird fly low over my head and vanish into a wall. I witnessed another *faqir* bilocate. I saw one *faqir*, who happened to be a dwarf, walk through a wall. Once during an *'imara*, in which for once I was not a participant, I watched Sidi Buzidi, the boss of the order's printing press, standing inside the circle conducting the dance as its *muqaddam*, and I distinctly saw smoke rising from his hands as he clapped out the beat. What the point of these visions was I do not know, but they did not bother me much at the time, or now for that matter. It was just the way things were in this holy place. I remember eavesdropping on a couple of *fuqara*: 'What's wrong with Ben Missoum?' 'Oh, he ate too many figs and had a vision in the middle of the night.' A *faqir* told me how he had drunk water that had poured out of an Islamic mandala, but this was 'not important. If you see a miracle, let it pass like a train before you and continue on the Road of Abandon.'

In an afterword to his novella *The Shadow Line* Joseph Conrad disparaged the supernatural:

The world of the living contains enough marvels and mysteries as it is – marvels and mysteries acting upon our emotions and intelligence in ways so inexplicable that it would almost justify the conception of life as an enchanted state. No, I am too firm in my consciousness of the marvellous to be ever fascinated by the mere supernatural, which (take it any way you like) is but a manufactured article, the fabrication of minds insensitive to the intimate delicacies of our relation to the dead and the living, in their countless multitudes; a desecration of our tenderest memories; an outrage on our dignity.

But for me my youth was a time of miracles, for I had seen the Shaikh al-'Alawi's tomb flash with light. And

Conrad seems to be indulging in some sort of epistemological snobbery.

In the days that followed my arrival, Faid set about discovering who I was by interrogating me about my dreams. It was a kind of holy psychoanalysis and while I was there I did indeed have many dreams that seemed pregnant with mystical meaning. One night I dreamed of a stranger to the town who entered the town's mosque but refused to perform any of the obligatory prayers. When the worshippers surrounded him and asked why he was not performing the prayers, he said nothing, but he began to change colour to a brilliant green like a light bulb – flesh, robes and skullcap – all of him bright green. Faid confirmed my guess that it was al-Khidr, a legendary figure who features in the Qur'an and who was the companion of Moses and is the guardian of the Well of Eternal Life. Faid said that he had entered my dream in order to destroy any reasons I had for staying attached to a particular religion. On another occasion I dreamed of the *Zawiya* as a hospital. The patient on the bed in the ward looked comfortable until one pulled back the blankets and saw that rotting sores – the marks of sin – pitted his body.

It was several days before I had an audience with Shaikh al-Mehdi. He lolled back wearing tinted glasses, a skullcap and a white robe. His head was shaven and he had a thin, ascetic body. He was not an extrovert and I did not know what to say to him. He had thin, stick-like arms and thin legs that I believe bore the marks of torture. (At this stage these were just the marks of torture by the French.) He always seemed to be concentrating intensely upon the matter in hand. His posture was flaccid, he was pale and did not look well. Later I heard that all three 'Alawi shaikhs had had problems with their wives. Later Faid told me that the reason that the Shaikh had taken a wife was to be tested and purified by the difficulties she made for him. Effectively

Faid was his tape recorder, memorising all his messages and then replaying them again and again.

The Shaikh spent a lot of time in the garage. He loved his Mercedes, cars in general, driving and mechanics and, if he had not become the Shaikh, he would have liked to have stayed a chauffeur. He used to go off on drives to escape the pressures of the *Zawiya*. As a youth he had worked as a chauffeur and had not even bothered to do the prayers. We used to touch his car for the *baraka* (blessing). Sometimes he watched television. From an article in *El Moudjahid*, the French-language national newspaper, I learned that when in 1952 Shaikh Hadj Adda, his adoptive father, died, al-Mehdi went into a coma for three days and three nights. When he came to, he found that he had been chosen to succeed as Shaikh of the *tariqa*. He was then only twenty-four. He had protested, but to no avail. (In medieval Europe that sort of thing was known as *nolo episcopari*, as men who were about to be consecrated as bishops made a show of wishing to refuse that honour.) He told his interviewer that during the war of liberation he had been militantly attached to the MTLD (Mouvement pour le Triomphe des Libertés Démocratiques). Anyway, after interrogating me for a while about my reason for coming to the *Zawiya*, he told me to listen to everything that Faid said. He gave me a *dhikr* and I will come back to that. He also told me to master the rituals of Islam and to read the Qur'an again and again, stopping only for prayers, meals and sleep.

At that stage I had only the most elementary knowledge of the background to the Qur'an. Equally crucially, I had no knowledge of or access to the vast body of exegetical literature developed over centuries to explain it. The only sort of training I had as any kind of exegete or glossator was being taught for A level how to read Shakespeare, Milton and Dickens. In the circumstances, the repetitive reading of the Qur'an was a curious experience. The book is quite short – shorter than the New Testament – so I found it possible to read the whole thing in a day. My reading in the broiling sun became a kind of fever. The powerfully rhythmic text was full of enigma, menace and mystical promises. Attempts to read it as a story, in the way that one can read a Gospel, were doomed to failure. Faced with obscurities in the Qur'anic text and true to the intellectual world that I had grown up in, I tried to supply my own meanings, based partly on my reading of the Sufi masters, but also on a half-baked knowledge of existentialism, Zen Buddhism and the ethos of Kerouac's *Dharma Bums*. The sacred text seethed with mysteries. What was an 'uncircumcised heart'? Who were 'the dwellers in the Thicket', who were 'evildoers'? What was 'the bird of omen' that God had fastened on every man's neck? What was the Holy screaming? The urgency of the messages – they had to be understood immediately – were like telegraph messages being dispatched to a battlefront. Occasionally I studied the Qur'an as I walked backwards and forwards on the roof, from where I could look down on the flat yellow roofs of the houses that tumbled in successive planes down to the sea.

I had the *fuqara* to instruct me, of course, and in the mosque I copied what they did. But the *Zawiya*'s printing press had also published a devotional manual, *Le Dogme de l'Islam*. This booklet stressed that in prayer one was talking to God and this had to be done with love. One stood with hands on one's chest while reciting a prayer which began '*Allahu akbar* ...' (God is great). When that short prayer was finished one raised one's hands and once again declared '*Allahu akbar*', before clasping one's hands in front of one's chest and reciting the *Fatiha*, the short opening chapter of the Qur'an, and then reciting the even shorter *Sura Iklhas* (The Chapter of Sincere Religion). Most Malikis – that is, most North African Muslims – perform that part of the prayer with their arms down their sides, but the 'Alawis

9. The prayer hall of the *Zawiya*

clasped their hands. Then one bowed, placing one's hands on one's knees as one did so, and recited '*Allahu akbar*' and '*Subhana rabbi al-'azim*' (Praise be to God the sublime). Then one straightened up into a new position … and so the prayer continued with short recitations and exaltations of God accompanied with a series of set movements. These included complete prostration with the face on the prayer mat and, finally, various gestures performed while in the kneeling position. The prayer certainly helped keep one fit and it reminded me a bit of physical education exercises at school, though, of course, the prayers were performed with far more gravity. According to Faid, the movements of the prayer are the yoga of Islam. I met several *fuqara* with a bump set between and a little above the eyes. They had acquired this bump from regular prostration in the prayer and I was told that it was actually the third eye. If one wore spectacles, one should take them off before performing the prayer, as the wearing of spectacles hindered the development of the third eye.

There were five daily prayers. *Subh* was the dawn prayer, which in summer was around half past four. I used to get up for it feeling horribly grey and cold. The disc of the sun appeared by the time one had completed this prayer. Breakfast was a hunk of coarse bread with a small cup of thick, sweet Turkish coffee. The sugar came from large cones that were knocked to bits with a hammer. It was de rigueur to swallow mouthfuls of bread and coffee taken together. Afterwards, this sparse breakfast might be supplemented by going up to a stall which opened at dawn and sold things that looked like ring doughnuts and which were cooked in hot oil. The *Zuhr* prayer took place very shortly after noon. The *'Asr* prayer took place at the moment when the sun was halfway between its zenith and its setting. There was a reading of the Qur'an after the *'Asr* prayer and in the course of a month the whole of the Qur'an was read out. The *Maghrib* prayer took place shortly after the disappearance of the sun (this was around seven in high summer) and the *Isha* prayer was performed after it had turned dark, approximately an hour and a half after sunset. There was often more chanting and poetry after the evening prayer. So I went to bed with the holy chanting dinning in my head.

Reunions of the *fuqara* to sing mystical chants took place regularly on Thursday evenings. On Fridays we went to the main mosque in town. At about half past eleven the Qur'an reading began, to be followed by a sermon and then the *khutba* (the declaration from the *minbar*, or pulpit, of the ruler of the country) and finally there were the noon prayers.

Just as it differs on points of law, so the North African Maliki way of doing the prayers differs slightly from that of the other three great law schools in Sunni Islam, the Shafi'i, the Hanafi and the Hanbali. The *fuqara* were not only diligent in performing the prescribed prayers, but also performed supernumerary prayers. Regular prayers, austere sleeping arrangements, poor food, lack of privacy, hard study and moral earnestness – it was rather like being back at public school again and yet I had been so pleased to leave my school only a year earlier.

Arabic as spoken in the *Zawiya* was a God-soaked language. When one started to eat or drink or commence any enterprise, one said '*bismillah*' (in the name of God). If things had worked out well it was '*al-hamdu l'illah*' (praise be to God). If there was some uncertainty about how something would work out, then it was '*in sha Allah*' (if God wills). If a *faqir* was bored, and there was a lot of boredom in the *Zawiya*, he was likely to express it with a long-drawn-out 'Allaaah'. And so on. The invocation of Allah came as naturally as breathing. According to Faid, one should always say '*bismillah*' at the climax of sexual orgasm. I think that my wife would punch me if I did that.

Faid introduced me to the '*imara*, or rather a kind of rehearsal for it, as an impromptu line of half a dozen of us with interlocked hands performed it in front of the Shaikhs' tombs one evening. We began by chanting '*La ilaha ila Allah*' (There is no god but God), then 'Allah', then '*huwa*' (He). Then this accelerated into '*hu*' (also He) and we swayed and bowed as we chanted. What had started up as a line changed to a closed circle and our feet beat upon the mats. At the end of it all I felt purified and at peace. I was told that I had done it well.

A few days later, on a Sunday, I performed a proper '*imara* in the company of about a hundred white-robed *fuqara*. Some of these were boys, but others were in their eighties. First, there was some preliminary chanting – haunting and very beautiful. Then, after the Shaikh had signalled his agreement to the *muqaddam*, everyone stood up. The dance was all a matter of instinct. Even I, a complete beginner, knew when the rhythm was going to change. A few *fuqara* did not participate, but stood outside the circle looking on. Those in the circle held hands. We leaned forward on the out-breath and returned to upright on the in-breath. The out-breath signified the destruction of the world and the in-breath its recreation. At every instant Allah destroys the world and then recreates it.

In the centre of the circle a couple of aged *fuqara* paced about and recited mystical verses composed by the Shaikhs of the 'Alawi *tariqa* or by other Sufis. From time to time they would beat out the rhythm or rearrange the clothing of one of the entranced dancers. There was a strong smell of sweat. The *'imara* was performed several times, I lost count how many, building repeatedly to a fierce and rapid climax and then resuming with what was once more initially a slow rhythm. The dancers ducked and swayed and bent at the knees, but then as the rhythm accelerated we stayed more upright as if we were pulled towards the heavens.

Occasionally a *faqir* would collapse on the ground in a fit. A person who had fallen victim to one of these scary fits was described as *melboos*. It was generally a sign that something was wrong in the person who was writhing on the ground. It was as if the dance was being invisibly policed by a fierce and vigilant spirit. Over the years, I went *melboos* several times and I found it a terrifying experience. It was as if something vast, alien and dispassionate was reaching into the heart of me to take me over. This was impossible to bear and hence the fits. It was, I suppose, a religiously induced form of epilepsy. After the dance, there was more chanting and glasses of mint tea were brought round. A collection was taken before we circled and embraced and kissed farewell. An outsider might guess that the *fuqara* danced in order to achieve ecstasy, but that would be a big mistake, for none of the *fuqara* needed a dance to reach ecstasy, nor were they seeking to achieve that state, and what one felt, if the dance had gone well, was not ecstasy but a sense of purification. Ecstasy was something that could strike in any place and at any time within the *Zawiya*. The *'imara* looks like and perhaps is a kind of war dance. At the end one hears the shuddering breaths, groans and wailing – all suggestive of a sense of failure and even death.

Later Faid told me that one should not put too much effort into the 'imara. When I performed it for the first time, I had done it without effort and that was right. 'You must let yourself relax in the 'imara. Bend the knees. Let them bend and let yourself follow, as if dying, and then you raise yourself, as if coming back to life. The 'imara is a sea in which one gets lost. The 'imara makes contact and then breaks it and so it purifies. This is much better than the whirling dance, for the Mevlevi whirling dance takes you to the level of the angels and leaves you there – that is simply an ecstasy – but the 'imara is much more and you notice that when you finish it you are not in ecstasy.' I learned from Ben Missoum that the correct etiquette for the 'imara was to keep the eyes downcast and almost closed.

In the Shaikh al-'Alawi's time, fuqara had been selected to undergo khalwa, a forty-day meditation in isolation in the desert or in a cave or, most often, in the tomb of one of the Shaikhs, during which the disciple recited a dhikr. Visions almost invariably ensued. However, khalwa had been discontinued by Hadj Adda, because he saw that the coming years would bring on a crisis of materialism, during which it would be too dangerous to practise this form of meditation. This way of approaching God had been closed and, as a consequence, in recent years some of the fuqara had lost spiritual ground. It was said that both Faid's 'heat' and his telepathic powers were due to his having spent too long in khalwa.

For meals, the men sat or knelt round communal bowls on low tables in a room just off the old mosque. (I had no idea how things were managed in the women's quarters, though I did hear that they spent a large part of every day getting rid of the little stones that would turn up in the bags of semolina from which the couscous was made.)

71

Lunch was *shorba*, a meatless stew of tomatoes with some unidentified greasy stuff poured over it, and a hunk of coarse bread. Dinner was always couscous with one or two skimpy-looking bits of mutton on top. With a pretence of politeness, one pushed particularly unappetising morsels round towards one's neighbour. Only hot chillies gave any real flavour. I remember thinking to myself one lunchtime, 'I know why I am feeling so strange here. It must be that the food is drugged.' Immediately, Faid burst out laughing. 'No, the food is not drugged,' he said, reading my mind as he so often did. On another occasion, Faid said, 'Here you don't eat the food. The food eats you.' During yet another lunch, he leaned over the communal bowl and said, 'People come here who have eaten Jesus, Moses and so on, but they cannot eat the couscous of the *Zawiya*.' Having lived on the stuff for weeks at a time, I am not surprised. Eventually the sight of a bowl of couscous began to sicken me. I am amazed that I can still enjoy the stuff today. Obviously, given the use of the left hand and water in the toilets, it was de rigueur to eat only with the right hand. One afternoon the following summer, Harvey told me that he had recently gone *melboos* (that is to say he had had what seemed to be a religiously inspired fit) listening to a Rolling Stones record and that he was going to ask Faid about it that evening, but he never got the chance to pop the question. As we sat hunched over the evening bowl of couscous, Faid started to hum a tune which he claimed was '*La Valse des Tueurs*' (The Waltz of the Killers), before explaining that all sorts of tunes and rhythms could provoke *melboos*, and then he started laughing. He claimed that many profane songs came from God. The content of our dinnertime conversation was frequently about Satan, the Messiah or the magic of Celtic place names. So, in retrospect, I suppose that as dinner table conversations go it was not too bad.

As instructed, I spent a great deal of time listening to

10. The exterior of the 'Alawi *Zawiya*

Faid. In his youth he had worked on tramp steamers on most of the world's oceans. During those voyages he had got to know lots of Yemeni sailors and through them he had learned about Islam and then taken the hand of the 'Alawi Shaikh. Many Yemenis were members of the 'Alawi order and I do not know if it still exists, but back in the sixties there was a Yemeni sailors' branch of the 'Alawi *tariqa* in Cardiff and an LP had been made of them performing the dervish dance. There were also branches of the 'Alawiya in South Shields and Birmingham. It was in the South Shields *Zawiya* that Faid had converted to Islam in 1943. Later, he had taken the hand of the Shaikh and settled in the Mostaganem *Zawiya* in 1962.

Faid believed fervently that Brittany was some kind of holy land and pondered the secret meanings of Breton place names. He was wild, comic and utterly mystical. He crammed his face full of food, demanded more coffee and kept talking of holy mysteries, whether anyone was listening or not. In the years that I knew him he developed cravings for French cowboy comics. He had a comic-book vision of holy history: 'And when Jesus saw the money changers in the Temple, Biff! Pow! Zokko! That's how he dealt with them!' Sometimes he thrust a comic book on me '*pour changer l'esprit un peu*'. It was impossible to take Faid seriously and yet it was impossible not to.

Faid taught by what he called *mudhakarat*, a mixture of anecdotes and holy sayings. 'It is very dangerous to do the *dhikr* when one is not pure. It is necessary to do the ablutions first.' When Faid had first performed the *dhikr*, his *murshid* (spiritual guide) seated him at the edge of a cliff and told him to say '*La ilaha ila Allah*' a hundred times. As Faid did so, his head began to turn and he saw his *nafs* (lower soul) rise out of him and commit suicide by hurling itself over the cliff. Then, 'Imagine you are in a garden. The *tariqa* is a garden with its trees, flowers and running water. But in the garden is a house with many chambers that you must enter and become familiar with. We can give you general directions to the house, but beyond that it is necessary that you should seek to discover the plan of the house yourself. We cannot help you. It is forbidden.' Then, 'If your heart tells you to go to the bistro and your head tells you to go to the *Zawiya*, go to the bistro, because you will find God in the bistro and the Devil in the *Zawiya*.' And so on. Faid was inexhaustible, but I was not. Later I was told of a man who agreed to be initiated by the Shaikh only on condition that he did not become like Sidi Abdullah Faid.

Faid told me not to spend too much time with the other *fuqara*. 'There is no need to talk to them. One comes here to smell the perfume of God.' Nevertheless I did talk to other *fuqara*. There was Abdullah Muslim Ben Qay, the one who drank water from an Islamic mandala. And saintly old Sidi Shuaib, who must have been in his eighties. And Ben Missoum, distinctive in a blue robe, who was peculiarly prone to *melboos* fits. And Dawud the halfwit, who got told off for doing the prayer too fast. And the saintly and very old 'Umar Labique, whose words were always accompanied by the clicking of the beads of his rosary as they passed through his hand. 'All is one. Names are only disguises,' he proclaimed. 'We are God. The infidel are God.' In his youth 'Umar had gone into *khalwa* and it was reported that he had never really come out of it. There was also the handsome, melancholy Abd al-Qadir, who wore a brown cowl in the Moroccan style. Faid remarked that his melancholy and his frequent illnesses came from Abd al-Qadir's fear of drowning.

A market stall in the square up the street from the *Zawiya* sold dirty postcards and luridly coloured pictures of Solomon and his Jinn and the Hand of Fatima with that sinister eye in the middle of the palm, as well as blurred photos of heroic FLN veterans. I had spotted a lot of

11. The Hand of Fatima, a talisman to avert the evil eye. One saw this image everywhere on the walls of the houses of Tijdit

pro-Ben Bella graffiti in Gouraya and the same was true in Mostaganem. Locals were not happy with the Boumedienne coup. I got the sense that only people in the big cities of Algiers and Oran were supporting Boumedienne. It was, of course, early days, but it was not long before people realised that Algeria was now being run by a corrupt and oppressive regime. The politicians of the FLN provided a skimpy veil for rule by the military and the Sécurité Militaire, and that rule was consolidated by the use of confiscations, murders, disappearances and torture. The regime's policy of confiscation and collectivisation was to wreck Algeria's agriculture. The regime, often referred to as *le Pouvoir* (the Power), also destroyed most of civil society by outlawing almost all forms of association that were not run by the FLN. In order to get anything serious done in that unhappy land, patronage and bribery were necessary.

Fanon, that false prophet, had written: 'After the war a disparity between the people and what is intended to speak for them will no longer be possible.' But in Mostaganem people were scared of walking on the pavement in front of the FLN headquarters. (On the other hand, there were lots of people who were just as scared of walking down the road between the two parts of the *Zawiya*.) In Tijdit there were frequent stand-offs between the police and the *fuqara*. Whenever the police came down the street with the intention of raiding the *Zawiya*, the *fuqara* would muster with knives and machetes (which otherwise they used for slaughtering sheep) and the police would retreat.

Ben Bella vanished from public view and it was not known what had become of him. A lot of the original leaders of the Algerian War of Independence, having fallen out of favour with the ruling regime, were arrested and disappeared, or, if they had taken refuge in Europe, they were assassinated there. The KGB and the Stasi brought the spies, thugs and torturers of the Algerian army up to professional standards, though of course the Algerian soldiers and FLN members had already learned quite a lot about torture from the French army. Various places were used for secret detentions. In Algiers those who were going to be subjected to violent interrogation were usually taken to the Antar Barracks in the Hydra district of the city. Favoured methods included the application of electrodes to the genitals, the chiffon technique, in which the victim was forced to drink vast quantities of dirty water which was poured through a cloth tied across his mouth, the *falaka*, or beatings on the soles of the feet, and suspension in handcuffs from the ceiling. But I only learned about these things much later. At this stage I knew almost nothing about Algerian history or politics.

I was taken by the *fuqara* out into the countryside to see the *Zawiya*'s experimental farm, Valley of the Gardens. The region was fertile and the farm produced apricots, mandarins, clementines, grenadines and figs. There were also docile cows and moulting peacocks. The Shaikh was keen on agriculture. I also visited the printing press of the *Zawiya* in Mostaganem proper. It did a lot of work for the government, printing tax forms and the like.

Days went by where nothing happened except prayer, meditation and religious instruction. Boredom alternated with ecstasy. Like body odours, ecstasy is something that nice people don't talk about, but the hell with that. From the first day I set foot in the *Zawiya* I was being eaten up by a kind of internal flame which lapped round the heart. Ecstasy starts in the heart, that is to say the left-hand side of the body. A fountain of fire within me threatened to tear me apart. Sometimes I found it difficult to stand. According to a tenth-century Iraqi Sufi, al-Junayd, ecstasy is 'a continual burning, a continual shaking to the foundations, a continual emptiness in which nothing familiar is ever seen, unimaginable and unbearable in its fierce onslaughts'. Over the centuries Sufi poets have used the (rather hackneyed) metaphor of drunkenness to evoke mystical ecstasy, but drunkenness and ecstasy are not the same. I have had enough experience of both to know the difference. There was perhaps a painful edge to the fiery experience of ecstasy, as if one's self, one's *nafs*, or lower soul, was being hollowed out. The *fuqara* called it *la presse* or *la presse intérieure*. It came without being sought for. It stayed with me sometimes for days and weeks at a time, sometimes for minutes only, and it left me as mysteriously as it came. It was like being eaten out from the inside. I have no idea what ecstasy is for. But Faid told me, '*Ton coeur a bougé beaucoup.*' Faid also said that one should not talk about one's interior experiences as that tended to hinder one's spiritual progress. On the other hand, one could sometimes speak about what one had experienced if this was intended to instruct others. So I have had no compunction regarding writing about it here.

It was important to receive authorisation for reciting a *dhikr*. There was one dervish who had recited a *dhikr* without permission and consequently he went mad for a while, banging his head against a wall and doing other strange things. But the Shaikh had given me a *dhikr* which I had to repeat thousands of times a day with my eyes shut. It was the *dhikr* customarily first given to disciples and the easiest for non-believers. It was a form of Hesychasm, but one done under supervision. At first when I recited it I had no belief in Allah. But soon I did. I suppose that it could be argued that I had succeeded in brainwashing myself. After, I think, six days in the *Zawiya* I decided to become a Muslim and not to return to England if the Shaikh so decreed. At this stage, I should note that there had been no pressure at all on me to convert. On the contrary, I was told that it really would be easier for me if I followed a Christian spiritual path.

And so things continued. For some weeks more I prayed, meditated and listened to Faid. Then suddenly I desperately wanted to get away. The Shaikh had told me not to leave without seeing him, but he was not granting me an audience. Despite my earlier resolution not to return to England if the Shaikh so decreed, I now felt an absolute need to disobey the Shaikh and go back to more familiar things. I loved the *fuqara* and the place, but at that stage I felt nothing for the Shaikh. Besides, I knew that my parents must be panicking madly about this venture into the unknown. I decided to flee one afternoon. I picked up a straw hat with a hole in it from a garbage dump beside the *Zawiya* and I was to wear it for much of the rest of the year. Apart from school caps, it was the first hat I ever owned. That evening, before walking on, I said goodbye to the boy who ran the lemonade stall in the same street as the *Zawiya*. 'You are mad, you know, Robert? What do you expect to do in Oran? You know the risks you run? Bandits, scorpions, even serpents.' I picked my way carefully across the gorge. The muezzin was making the evening call as I fled Mostaganem. I had five dinars in my pocket as I started walking along the coast road towards Arzew and Oran.

I remember walking out late under the stars, sheath knife at hand, on the road to Oran. Palm trees flanked the road. The land on either side stretched flat to the horizon and the wild dogs bayed from skyline to skyline. I did not know why I was going or why I was going then, but it felt like another of those rare moments of shaping destiny. I walked some fifteen kilometres before lying down to an uneasy sleep on the edge of a vineyard. I rose with the sun and very soon a lorry offered me a lift all the way into Oran. But there my troubles began. It would be tedious to go into detail, but all the banks were closed and I encountered many difficulties as I was directed from place to place. In order to get rid of colonial ghosts, Algeria's revolutionary government had renamed most of the streets, but without bothering to tell their inhabitants. I had no money to buy a ticket for a boat or for somewhere to stay. Somehow this all got sorted out and the following day the boat, *Ville de Tunes*, left quite punctually half an hour late. On arrival in Marseilles, because I was British, a sailor rushed me to join the first-class passengers waiting for disembarkation. It was the Arabs' turn to queue. In France my traveller's cheques worked and I could buy food. I hitched back to Paris, where in the Gare de l'Est I bought myself a platform ticket and slept in the Salle d'Attente and, when gendarmes tried to turf me out, I faked a nosebleed.

At the end of *Homage to Catalonia* George Orwell describes how strange it seemed, after returning from the Spanish Civil War, to be travelling through the south of England on a train:

Down here it was still the England I had known in my childhood: the railway-cuttings smothered in wild flowers, the

80

deep meadows where the great shining horses browse and meditate, the slow-moving streams bordered by willows, the green bosoms of the elms, the larkspurs in the cottage gardens; and then the huge peaceful wilderness of outer London ...

It was like that for me too, except that, as my train entered the outer wilderness of the metropolis, I fell to imagining the impact that the scale and wealth of London would make on my friends in Mostaganem. They were mostly untra-velled, unworldly and desperately poor. I had journeyed between two mutually unimaginable worlds.

12. Noah and his Ark

4

SACRED AND PROFANE LOVE

IT WAS NOW THE AUTUMN TERM of 1965. I returned to Oxford as from a strange dream that had lasted months. A friend in Corpus Christi looked at me and said, 'Excuse me, but you are Robert Irwin, aren't you?' I was almost unrecognisable. My hair was long, I had started a beard and I was tanned. My face had changed, I had a hungry ascetic look and my eyes were searching distant horizons. I was thinner than ever thanks to the diet at the *Zawiya*, hitchhiking, parsimony and dysentery. I had elected to switch from National Health specs to the sort of heavy, black-framed things that advertising executives were supposed to wear in the fifties and sixties. Also, I had acquired a lot of polonecked pullovers (as popularised by Colin Wilson). I wore a ring with a skull on its bezel and one day a stranger in the street accosted me and asked if it was my family crest.

I tried to explain to a few friends what I had seen and felt in Mostaganem. But mostly I talked to Harvey. The second time we talked we started comparing experiences at midnight and finished at a quarter to seven in the morning. Harvey's experience of Mostaganem had been less ecstatic than mine as he had had dysentery most of the time he

83

was there, but he thought that it was possible that he had had 'holy dysentery', something that he had to go through in order for his metabolism to adjust to mystic states. The Shaikh had told Harvey to work at washing bottles while he was still very ill from dysentery, but when the Shaikh gave anyone a job of work, he gave them the strength to carry it out.

Harvey and I continued to argue about everything. Harvey, though an anarchist, thought that it would be a mistake to assassinate Franco and that the Catalans were not worth improving. He also thought that the Nuremberg war trials had been illegal. But we agreed that happiness could not be an ultimate value – which was good, because neither of us was particularly happy. One of Harvey's theories was that the planet earth was a disguised mental asylum. Given the people we both knew, this was not a surprising theory. When I argued in favour of changing the world for the betterment of humanity, he countered that he did not believe that human beings exist.

I had moved into new rooms in college. My previous room had been small, dark and bleak, but now I stepped down into my new airy and spacious suite. I shared a staircase and a lavatory with the famous Chaucerian scholar Neville Coghill. At that time he was busy advising on a film version of Marlowe's *Doctor Faustus*, starring Richard Burton and Elizabeth Taylor. (When she visited Merton, I remember thinking that she was looking much more attractive than when she impersonated Cleopatra.) From one of the windows of my new rooms I could walk out on to the lawn, where there was a mulberry tree which had been planted in the seventeenth century and an armillary sundial. I sat reading medieval texts on the grass and I took it for granted that these beautiful surroundings were my scholarly due.

In the autumn term, after an anarchist meeting, Harvey

and I staged an impromptu performance of the *'imara* in the quadrangle of Corpus Christi. Barefoot, some of us in leather jackets and some wearing scarves in red and black (the colours of anarchism), we commenced the slow invocation of the name of God. The dance became faster and noisier. Windows above us flew open and our performance reached its climax after someone at one of the windows poured a bucket of water over us. Dispassionate observers commented that the dance seemed very sexual.

> *Black and red together, we shall not be moved.*
> *Anarchy forever, we shall not be moved.*

The Oxford proctors insisted that in order for the Anarchist Society to be sanctioned by the authorities and be able to publicise itself at things like the Freshers' Fair, it had to have a constitution and a subscription. We conformed. So the subscription became a penny per annum and each member of the Anarchist Society was president for a day. (Somehow this reminds me of G. K. Chesterton's marvellous novel *The Man Who Was Thursday*.) Ex-public school boys predominated in the Anarchist Society (though Harvey was an exception) and we ex-public school boys had radically different views about the value of the public schools' Officer Training Corps. Some, like me, had taken it for granted that it was our duty to rebel against military discipline by marching out of step, firing at one's neighbour's target, wearing a CND badge in one's beret and so forth, but there were others who had worked hard on their orienteering and marksmanship, confident that these would be useful skills when the bloody revolution came. I dithered between the violent anarchism of Nechayev and the pacifist anarchism of Tolstoy and Kropotkin, though I tended towards the latter. My anarchism had been a natural response to the previous regimen at my school, where almost everything that was not compulsory was forbidden. We invited speakers to come and talk to us and I remember that we barracked the 'anarchist' Sir Herbert Read for accepting a knighthood. We liaised with a genuine anarchist commune in Witney where the children ran wild and the parents looked harassed. In the long run, I had to give up anarchism as I could not explain to anyone, including myself, how it could work.

Anarchism was an extreme position, but rebellion was in the air and so many films of the era celebrated young (and, in retrospect, rather repulsive) rebels: Morgan in *Morgan, a Suitable Case for Treatment*, Billy in *Billy Liar* and Benjamin in *The Graduate*. (I will come to *If …* later.) We were against war, sexual prudery, censorship, bourgeois values, but above all against parents. In retrospect, I am sad that we gave our parents such a hard time and that those films had encouraged us to do so. Like so many adolescents, I was obsessively self-preoccupied and I had no interest in the lives of my parents, though I now see that they had had a more interesting and even more romantic life than I have had.

My mother is Dutch and, since she was daughter of the Queen of Holland's notary, she grew up in the company of the children of ship-owning and art-collecting millionaires. She did a finishing course in Switzerland, where she learned cordon bleu cookery. Then, shortly before the outbreak of the Second World War, she married a German count and went off to live in a castle, where she looked after the children of his first marriage. But things did not work out in the way that they do in *The Sound of Music* and in the middle of the war she got divorced and returned to Holland, to a large house in Capelle-aan-den-Ijssel, where my grandfather was hiding Jews in the attic. Like most Dutch people, her family endured great privations during the war and she was reduced to eating tulip bulbs. When eventually the

British and their allies arrived, a dance was held in the local-
ity. There a Canadian air force man was trying to feel her up
when a British medical officer, who looked a bit like Clark
Gable, stepped up and asked, 'Madam, is this man pester-
ing you?' When my mother nodded yes, the medical officer
knocked the Canadian out. That officer became my father.
He went on to become a consultant psychiatrist and treated
many famous people, including Tony Hancock. Eventually my father rose to become Superintendent of Holloway
Sanatorium, where he presided most reluctantly over that
great institution's closure. As for my Dutch grandfather, he
lost almost all his fortune investing in something daft like
Argentinian swamp railways. He was reflecting on how he
was going to have to give all his staff notice when he saw
that they were passing a newsagent's. On an impulse he told
his chauffeur to stop and he went into the newsagent's and
bought a lottery ticket. He won the national state lottery
and from that he rebuilt his fortune and he never had to fire
the chauffeur.

Though my brother and I were given excellent and
expensive educations, we both went off the rails at about
the same time and we were certainly a cause of grief and
anxiety to my parents in the sixties. They could not understand my flight into Islam. On the other hand, I do not
think that they tried very hard. I guess they thought that it
was a phase I was going through. I know that we had some
terrible rows, but my memory has erased the detail of what
was said in them. As the fourteenth-century philosopher-
historian Ibn Khaldun observed, 'Each man resembles his
own times more than he does his father.'

I continued to read what I could about Sufism, but there
was not a great deal to read in English and much of what there
was had been produced by René Guénon, Frithjof Schuon,
Titus Burckhardt and Martin Lings, all of whom were
believers in an ancient Perennial Wisdom. In time, I came

to regard all their writings with suspicion. René Guénon (1886–1951) was and is a famous figure in France, but he is much less well known in Britain and America. Raised as a Catholic, he had studied under a charlatan called Papus, the Grand Master of the occult Martinist order, but Guénon soon became disillusioned and moved on to an obsessive and long-lasting engagement with Freemasonry. He quested for an ancient Primordial Tradition that was pure of contamination by the West's debased, largely secular values. In 1910 he met Ivan Aguéli, a Swedish painter who had received a Sufi initiation in Egypt and whose Sufism relied heavily on the teaching of the thirteenth-century Andalusian mystic Ibn al-Arabi. Aguéli had been initiated by Shaikh 'Abd al-Rahman al-Kabir, an Egyptian Shadhili. In 1912 Guénon converted to Islam, taking the name Shaikh Abd al-Wahid Yahya. Finally, in 1930 he took up residence in Egypt, where he lived as a Muslim and Shadhili Sufi.

Why did Guénon become a Muslim? As he saw it, there was no choice, since he was obsessed with the importance of initiation, which in his eyes took precedence over all other aspects of religion, and he denied the initiatic quality of the debased Christian sacraments. He would have liked to have become a Hindu, but Hindu initiation was closed to him, since he belonged to no caste. Buddhism might have been an option, but, at the time he was looking for an initiation, he still thought of Buddhism as a Hindu heresy. So his choice of Islam was very much *faute de mieux* and, despite his formal adherence to Islam, he continued to write about the Vedanta, which he celebrated as the most direct expression of pure metaphysics. Like Schuon and the rest of the Perennialists, he believed in transcendent unity of all the major religious traditions, though this unity could only be properly intuited by a spiritual elite. Religions, in their exoteric forms, as understood by ordinary worshippers, are distorted forms of the Perennial or Primordial Wisdom.

Guénon was a prolific producer of books and articles whose crankiness must be obvious to anyone who has half a brain. He wrote about the ancient science of palmistry; about the martyrdom of the Templars and how the Freemasons were the degenerate heirs of the Templars. In an article 'Roi du Monde' (in *Les Cahiers du mois*, 1925), he instructed his readership about Agarttha, a secret place in the Himalayas which was the spiritual centre of the world and the seat of the King of the World and supreme pontiff. (A peculiar light given off the rocks allowed the millions of subterranean citizens of Agarttha not only to see their way around, but also to grow vegetables.)

Guénonism is elitist. Guénon opened his *The Reign of Quantity and the Signs of the Times* (1945) with the observation: 'It is scarcely necessary to say that everything that the author has set out in this book and elsewhere is intended to be addressed exclusively to these few, without any concern for the incomprehension of others ...' Like many esotericists, he despised the materialistic West and its 'Reign of Quantity'. Only in the Orient was there any chance of making contact with a living spiritual tradition. It was, after all, to Asia that the Rosicrucians had fled after the Thirty Years War, or so he imagined. Since he despised the human individual, women's rights, democracy, science and progress, it is not surprising that he influenced fascist writers like Drieu la Rochelle and Julius Evola. 'Hitler? He is Guénon with Panzer divisions' was one of Evola's half-serious jokes. Still, it is surprising that the left-wing Surrealist André Breton took Guénon seriously.

As for Schuon, he deplored the Allied victory in 1945 as the victory of the profane over something more ancient. Like Guénon, he had dabbled with Freemasonry in his youth. Like Guénon, he was not happy with the age he was living in: 'For conservative intellectuals, Islam is the only space in which the Industrial Revolution has not yet happened.' Schuon first heard of al-'Alawi from Arab sailors in Marseilles and in 1932 he took a boat from there to Oran and made his way to Mostaganem, where he was eventually initiated by Shaikh al-'Alawi. In his splendid book *Against the Modern World: Traditionalism and the Secret Intellectual History of the Twentieth Century*, Mark Sedgwick describes Schuon's first visit:

> Schuon spent three months in this way, living in a room in the Zawiya furnished only with a straw mat, a mattress, and blanket. In addition to talking to other Alawis, he spent time walking on the beach, and after the ritual prayer at sunset would stand in the courtyard outside the mosque to admire the poignant beauty of the scene. This routine is fairly normal for a new arrival in a Sufi order, who in this way becomes part of the community centered around the shaykh, learning from that community by example as well as through casual conversation, taking time to digest and internalize the whole experience.

(Yes, that is exactly what it was like.)

In 1933 Schuon made two further trips to Mostaganem in preparation for setting up a Sufi group in France. Shaikh Hadj Adda made him a *muqaddam* (roughly 'supervisor') and, according to one reading, this meant that Schuon had the authority to initiate others into Sufism. Faid told me that Schuon had reached a point in the *Zawiya* where it had become too strong for him. He had become a great shaikh, but the Shaikh Hadj Adda told him that he had to leave. Schuon used his authority as *muqaddam* to create a breakaway group of European Sufis and, with the help of Titus Burkhardt, a rather vapid and woolly writer on esoteric aspects of Islam, set up *khanqah*s in Paris and Lausanne. ('*Khanqah*' is a word of Persian origin and it means pretty much the same as *zawiya*.) When, in 1946, Hadj Adda died,

13. Shaikh al-'Alawi's successor, Shaikh Hadj Adda Bentounes

Schuon was acclaimed by his followers as Shaikh. He and his group had effectively broken away from the 'Alawiya. Later, Schuon made Martin Lings his *muqaddam* in Britain. Schuon started by being intransigently dogmatic on Islam. For example, he wrote:

The intellectual – and thereby the rational – foundation of Islam results in the average Muslim having a curious tendency to believe that non-Muslims either know that Islam is the truth and reject it out of pure obstinacy, or else are simply ignorant of it and can be converted by elementary explanations; that anyone should be able oppose Islam with a good conscience quite exceeds the Muslim's imagination, precisely because Islam coincides in his mind with the irresistible logic of things.

But later Schuon drifted on to other enthusiasms and his once rigorous Islam became diluted by alien doctrines. He presided over a secretive and Westernised version of Sufism. The secretiveness derived from that of the Freemasons and other occultist groups with whom Guénon and Schuon were familiar, and this secretive elitism was in strong contrast with the social inclusiveness of the 'Alawiya in Mostaganem, Paris, Cardiff and elsewhere. Schuon came to believe that he had gained the spiritual vision to detect the Primordial Wisdom in a variety of ancient traditions and that he had the authority to construct what was in effect a new religion that was only nominally Sufi. He eventually fell out with Guénon and others because he held it was not necessary to observe all the laws and rituals of Islam, since there was a need to adapt 'to the conditions of life in the West'. He also recruited Christian followers and he told his Muslim followers that it was permissible to drink beer to conceal one's Islam.

Schuon had been another of the people whom Zaehner had attacked in *Mysticism, Sacred and Profane*, for being an advocate 'of a *philosophia perennis* which would set itself above creed and which therefore interprets all creeds from its own *a priori* notions'. Also, Zaehner, determined to refute Schuon on the primacy of Islam, sought to demonstrate that Christ was the fulfilment of all religious revelations, including those of the Arab world, India and Iran.

Zaehner described Schuon as 'a kind of super-Pope' who presided over a 'higher mystification'. Later, after I stopped reading Schuon's books and, for that matter, Zaehner's, Schuon moved to the United States. I will return to Schuon in the penultimate chapter. His end was not good.

Though my head was filled with mystical madness, I did work and I produced my essays on time and to a high standard, as was expected, since I had been awarded a major scholarship. I used a college prize to buy an Arabic–English dictionary. Ever since I was a small boy I had been interested in the Crusades. Like so many medievalists of my generation, I had been seduced by Steven Runciman's cadenced prose and vivid picture painting. And in their book *Crusader Castles* Robin Fedden and John Thomson had described Crac des Chevaliers in Syria so evocatively:

> Today Krak of the Knights, so perfectly preserved, seems incongruously empty, its silence hardly natural. The windmill that stood upon the north wall should be grinding corn; in the huge vaulted chamber ... that must once have housed the men-at-arms, troops should be quartered; the cry of the watch should echo along the battlements; and in the halls and passages the clank of mailed knights; the guardroom should be noisy with medieval French, and from the chapel should come the chant of the Latin mass. Instead there are only the shadows of the kestrels cruising above, and the sun-scorched stones.

Names like Tancred of Antioch, Raymond of Oultrejourdain and Balian of Ibelin used to roll around in my head. Naturally, that interest intensified as I found myself studying in depth the Crusaders, Europeans who had encountered Islam centuries before I had. I felt the call of the East from centuries ago.

In Merton, Roger Highfield's and John Roberts's tutorial styles differed from that of Davis and from each other, but all three were excellent teachers. However, university lectures were of a more variable quality. I went to hear Robert Graves when he was Oxford Professor of Poetry and his lectures were crazy and full of stuff about the White Goddess. I heard Isaiah Berlin on the history of political thought and, bored, I took my notes in a visual comic-strip form. I also heard K. B. McFarlane on the Lancastrian nobility, Marie-Thérèse d'Alverny on the transmission of Islamic science to the West, Beryl Smalley on the Albigensian heresy, Tom Boase on Crusader castles, Lorenzo Minio-Palluelo on Dante and so on. My friends and I scoured the lecture lists for esoteric subjects. The expert on Buddhist predicate logic, who lectured beside his cardboard coffin, was the winner here. His lectures consisted of strange incantatory stuff about pot, lightning and space and about which of the three logically fitted into which (so it was a bit like that game, Scissors, Stone, Paper). Almost the entire class sat mesmerised, but stifling their giggles.

I continued to encounter bizarre people, including John Brodie. He used to collect second-hand books on coal mining, for no better reason than that they were always so cheap. He told us that he wished to drop litter in the street to express his alienation from straight society, but that he found he did not have enough emotional energy for such a simple defiant act. 'Why is "packed with lethargy"' not an expression in the English language?' he asked me once. On one of his walls I read, 'A physicist is composed of atoms. A physicist is an atom's way of finding out about atoms.' One evening he turned to Harvey and, nodding his head in my direction, said, 'I don't know about you, but he terrifies me.'

Kittoo, my Indian friend at Keble, was a Buddhist who had a meditation master in London, someone from the Theosophical Society, I think, who used to levitate before

Kittoo's eyes, but later he was taught by his guru in his sleep. Before he gave all his property away, friends found him weeping in his room in Keble after he had taken the sins of the world upon himself. It was also Kittoo who exorcised a launderette on Walton Street using a Tibetan ritual exorcism knife. I cannot remember why the place needed exorcising. Then there was Sarah, who wanted to knit woolly socks for the American troops in Vietnam, but also dreamed of becoming an anchorite. She was haunted by the ghost of a former boyfriend, who at night lay heavily breathing on her floor.

I met John Aiken after the meeting of the Buddhist Society which had been addressed by Christmas Humphreys. On our first encounter John Aiken told me that the Buddha would be reincarnated in six million years' time; that he knew a stigmatic hysteric in Liverpool; that he, John Aiken, could create lines on his thumbnails by sheer mental power; that it was not a good idea to be reincarnated after only a short interval as, in order to make spiritual progress, one would get more benefit from being reincarnated in a totally different sort of society. He smiled all the time he told me these things. John's powerful intellect had run wild on the fringes of knowledge. He had a photographic memory and he was the expert on the Clear Light, Tantric sex, flying saucers, *stukas*, lamas, astrology, DNA and Hondas. He told me that 'To have died on a motorbike is the noblest way of perishing for those in *samsara*.' He once rushed into a neighbour's room in St Catherine's, shouting, 'I'm high! I'm high! I'm high!' Pause. 'Yes, I'm high on two marvellous drugs, air and water.' He then squeezed a bicycle pump and declared it to be lovely music. Which reminds me of Rip Blake, the undergraduate who had hosted our dervish dance in Corpus. One night he burst into the room of a student on the same staircase who was asleep, shouting, 'Do you realise what time it is? It is three o'clock in the morning!'

Occasionally, to wind my visitors up, I used to preach the values of middle-class life and bourgeois morality as the estimable product of many centuries of social evolution. Families and everyday pastimes were beautiful. My words were shocking. It was as if I had farted loudly in an enclosed space.

Through her eerily brilliant son Ben, I met Freda Wint, not a student but a resident of Park Town and a leading figure in Friends of the Western Buddhist Order. She told me that, while giving birth to Ben, she had had a vision of being surrounded by a ring of Buddhas. From time to time, she became a recluse and pretended not to be in Oxford. Years previously she had created a *tulpa*, a thought form created by intense visualisation, which got out of control. She had worked on a shadow on the wall until it became a seventeenth-century gentleman. As *tulpa*s do (and see the writings of Alexandra David-Neel on this), the *tulpa* developed a mind of its own and was threatening to kill her children, including my friend Ben. Suddenly she turned on it and said, 'Why, you are me!' and it promptly disintegrated. She reckoned that it was an *animus* figure, a male phantasm that she had projected. She had spent time in a Buddhist monastery in Thailand and while she was there she told her friend that she was going to ask her master three questions, though she did not say what those questions were. That evening in hall the master stood up and said, 'I do not answer questions. That is not my function, nor do I read minds.' He then proceeded to deal with Freda's three questions. Over the next few years she worried about me and gave me a long talking-to about not leaving Oxford in order to follow a spiritual path. Devout Buddhist though she was, she was certain that it was better to get a degree before bothering about more mystical matters.

The godgame nonsense continued. *The Godgame* was John Fowles's title for what he eventually published as *The*

Magus in 1966. Having read a highly critical, downbeat review of this novel in the *Guardian*, I knew that this was the book I had been waiting for all my life and I went out and bought it in the first week of publication; it was the first hardback novel I ever bought. Nicholas Urfe arrives on the Greek island of Phraxos to take up a teaching post there. He soon encounters a millionaire, Maurice Conchis, and is entertained in his luxurious villa. Led on by the beautiful Lily Montgomery, who first appears as a ghost and later as an alleged mental patient of Conchis, Nicholas falls victim to Conchis's manipulative lies and charades. Again and again, what passes for reality in the villa turns out to have a false bottom. Psychodrama, Russian roulette, an aristocracy of the spirit, voyeurism and masked rituals feature in a programme of deceit designed to educate Nicholas in the true nature of love. Eventually judged to be fit for life, he emerges from a labyrinth of illusions and leaves the island. Moreover, like Lawrence Durrell's *Alexandria Quartet*, *The Magus* chronicled a progressive initiation under a Mediterranean sun. This then was no mere novel, for it was a guide to the Meaning of Life – but unfortunately a rather enigmatic one.

> When the mode of the music changes, the walls of the city shake.
>
> (Plato, *The Republic*)

I discovered pop music in 1966. Previously I had hated it. At school the same records had been played again and again on the house record player – Elvis Presley, Buddy Holly and Connie Francis – and I vociferously hated the twanging guitars and the maudlin lyrics. I affected to prefer Schoenberg, Varèse and the chanting of Buddhist priests. Frank Sinatra once described rock as 'martial music for every side-burned delinquent on the face of the earth'. But in the autumn of 1966 a friend in Oxford put the Beatles's

Revolver on the turntable and for the first time I found myself listening to something that I thought could seriously be compared with classical music. Indeed, 'Eleanor Rigby' certainly owed something to Vivaldi, just as 'Penny Lane' was a consequence of Paul McCartney having listened to Bach's Brandenburg Concerto. The Beatles's lyrics about loneliness and desolation appealed to me, the use of sitar and tabla evoked the psychedelic and I heard the call of the Orient in some of the tracks.

But essentially this Oxford year, which ran from autumn 1965 to the summer of 1966, was a year in suspended animation, as I was waiting for the summer and the possibility of returning to Mostaganem. I felt homesick for Algeria. Before I left England again in the summer of 1966, I dreamed that I moved among the vines with my companions and gathered in the grape harvest under an ink-blue night sky. I had a grant from my college to explore the Islamic lands and I reached Mostaganem by a circuitous route. I took a train to Istanbul and then hitched from Istanbul to Damascus (which I reached in a single lift). From Damascus I carried on to Jordan and made my way to Jerusalem (which was then still in Jordanian hands). In the Holy Sepulchre I burst into tears for no obvious reason. Then I hitched back up and across to Beirut, from where I took a Russian boat to Alexandria. I hitched across the Egyptian and Libyan deserts with some difficulty. On one occasion my lift dumped me in a featureless part of the Sahara from which I was rescued by passing American oilmen. The wreckage of the Second World War was still everywhere in the desert and scrap-metal merchants padded around burnt-out tanks. I made my way out of the Kingdom of Libya into Tunisia and then travelled along the coastline to Mostaganem. I had slept in assorted youth hostels, in a farmyard, in the back of a lorry, in a gypsy encampment, on the beach, in a gutter in Tunis and in an Algerian police station. I had had lots of vivid dreams, most of which I carefully recorded. By now I was a lean, tough and practised traveller. I felt that I was purified by the heat and I was fanatical.

This time when I turned up in Mostaganem there were fewer *pieds noirs* in the main square. I wasted no time in Mostaganem proper, but hurried on to the *Zawiya*. The minute I walked into the courtyard I experienced that same heavy atmosphere that had worked so strangely on my spirit the previous year. Soon after my arrival I had an audience with the Shaikh. I never knew what to say to him. He seemed worried that Harvey had not arrived with me. He said that Harvey had a special *maqam* (rank) and that he needed to come to the centre. The Shaikh said that I should be left free and without constraint. A day or two later I learned that he had announced to the *fuqara* who were with him that I understood neither Moses, Jesus nor Muhammad. He said that I understood nothing. The Shaikh avoided directly questioning visitors to the *Zawiya*, but as soon as they were gone, he took soundings from those *fuqara* who had spent time with the visitors. If the Shaikh was a mirror to all men, as Faid had hinted, then I saw myself as complex, enigmatic and frightening. Most of the *fuqara* were indeed, what their name implied, poor, but the Shaikh also had wealthy disciples and people who were in influential positions, even within the FLN, were also his followers.

Sidi Ben Daish was the Shaikh's *muqaddam*, which is to say that he was the Shaikh's deputy and effectively the manager of the *Zawiya*. Whenever he saw the Shaikh, he took evil from him and received nothing, for the Shaikh said that he could not give Ben Daish anything. (But I can no longer remember what Ben Daish looked like. He is a wraith in my head.)

That summer I was put to work in the printing press with two or three of the young *fuqara*. It was only fair that I

14. Shaikh al-Mehdi, my initiator in the 'Alawi order

should earn my keep. The work of putting one calendar date on top of another was so monotonous that I was able to read French novels as I slapped page on page. Thus, as my hands toiled away, my eyes devoured Sarraute, Robbe-Grillet and Camus. (The newsagent in Mostaganem sold me novels by these authors. Would that there was a newsagent like that in south London today.) From time to time I found the ecstasy was burning within so fiercely that I had to stop working and wait for it to pass. Ecstasy and existentialist novels apart, it was jolly boring working at the printing press. So there was a lot of conversation among the young *fuqara* who worked beside me. We talked not about spiritual matters, but about Françoise Hardy and Sylvie Vartan, the bizarre Scottish habit of wearing kilts, the Beatles, Stones and Elvis and how my new friends needed to get jeans from London. They read the French pop culture magazine *Salut les copains*, as well as the French equivalent of *Brides Monthly*, and they were desperate to get hold of a pair of blue jeans, or, better yet, to get a French work permit.

The lads were also keen on *shema* and tried to teach me how to spit the stuff out properly (as previously noted, the Algerians are marvellous spitters). *Shema*, also known as *shammah*, is Algerian mouth tobacco and consists of a mixture of tobacco, powdered carbonate of lime, ash, black pepper and oils. From a little silver circular tin with a crescent and a star on its lid, a pinch of the moistly reeking stuff is taken and rammed into the space between the gum and the cheek and the effects are felt within seconds. Its burn offered a fantastically powerful nicotine effect and, when it was at its freshest, I found it difficult to stand upright. But after five or ten minutes one had to get rid of the stuff and hence the spitting, though in later years back in Britain I discreetly used a Kleenex. I was addicted to *shema* for about fifteen years. It made my mouth taste horrible, but it kept me slim and consoled me in bad times. A little later in the sixties I ran into another freak who had been in Afghanistan who told me that there *shema* was called *naswa* and the Afghan tins had little mirrors on the top so that the Afghans could see where the *naswa* was in their mouth. Eventually a male nurse warned me that I was running the serious risk of getting mouth cancer and so, in the course of two or three irritable weeks, I gave up.

I still have a page from one of those calendars that I was compiling in the press. I found it recently in my copy of the old Penguin edition of Flecker's *Hassan* that I used to travel with. 'If a man could pass through Paradise in a dream, and have a flower presented to him as a pledge that his soul had really been there, and if he found that flower in his hand when he awoke – Aye, and what then?' (Coleridge, *Anima Poetae*).

A few days after I had been put to work Harvey arrived in town. Late one afternoon he walked in on the printing press on the way to the *Zawiya* and we hugged. Then we took the bus to Tijdit. Harvey had news about the latest Beatles release, 'Yellow Submarine', though he was pretty disparaging about it. We were guilty about our debauched and intellectual lives at Oxford. Soon after Harvey arrived, Faid asked him if he said the prayers in England. Harvey, embarrassed, gestured no. 'That does not matter. Only we are obliged to ask.'

If I was mad, then Harvey was mad with me – folie à deux. He spoke repeatedly about the cone of annihilation and I went on to have dreams about this dreadful cone. After Harvey left the *Zawiya* the previous year, he had a dream in which the Shaikh ordered two of the *fuqara*, Omar and 'Abd al-Salam, to be killed. Faid interpreted that as meaning that Harvey was coming to regard those two *fuqara* too highly. At one point Harvey had written to the Shaikh saying that there was no God and he could understand nothing. One thing puzzled Faid. He was certain that Harvey was a *majdhub*, but yet he never cried out, which was odd, for Faid and all the other *majdhub*s that he knew cried out on being touched, and they did the same on hearing violent noises. (In fact, Harvey did feel the need to shout when he was touched, but he tried to cut it down as much as possible in company.) 'You have the manner of a *majdhub*,' Faid told Harvey. 'What you get, you receive from the other *fuqara*, but they do not feel what you feel. This is the *tariqa* working upon you. But the *tariqa* cannot leave you like this. It is obliged to tie you to the earth a little.' (By the way, a *majdhub* is not an entirely desirable thing to be. The local children made no distinction between holy fools and the ordinarily insane and they indiscriminately threw stones at both sorts.)

Harvey asked Faid about the *'imara*, for each time he performed it, a seizure came upon him and he rolled about on the ground and screamed. He was told to approach the Shaikh when he was on his own and ask for his authorisation to perform the *'imara*.

While at the *Zawiya*, Harvey worked at his Arabic and he compiled word lists and transcribed prayers. Though at this stage I could not follow him in studying the language, I planned to do so in the future, for learning Arabic would be more than acquiring a foreign language. It would be an act of piety, as it would put me in direct contact with the word of God. But I delayed, because there were difficulties. In the first place I could not decide which Arabic to master, classical, modern standard or Algerian colloquial?

Besides, practically everybody in Algeria spoke French. The government was trying to discontinue the teaching of French, as it wanted to promote Arabic as the language of national unity, but at this point it was not having much success, partly because there were not enough trained teachers of Arabic. Those Algerians who could read preferred a French-language newspaper like *El Moudjahid* to any of the

Arabic-language journals. The Berbers and Kabyles resisted having Arabic forced upon them and sometimes they did so with violence. So I got along fine with French and it was disconcerting to realise that something I had studied at school for O level was actually useful to me. For the time being, the only Arabic I memorised by heart apart from some simple salutations were the words of the *shahada* and the prayers, as well as four of the shortest *sura*s of the Qur'an.

Having given away my copy of *A Moslem Saint of the Twentieth Century* to the *fuqara* the previous year, I had purchased another copy and this I read and reread and I found in it enigmatic messages that came from another world. Al-'Alawi once told a disciple, 'Life is not one of your attributes, for you are dead in the form of the living, just like a possessed madman who claims to be someone he is not.' According to al-'Alawi, one of the attributes of God was pure nothingness. Again, 'The Outwardly manifest is veiled by nothing but the strength of its manifestations.' (I have modernised these quotations from Lings's book, for I do not see why twentieth-century Sufis should be made to talk like early Victorian poets.)

I continued to study the Qur'an and to recite a *dhikr*, recitation of words in praise of Allah. *Wird* strictly means a specified time of day or night set aside for private worship, but in the context of the *Zawiya*, it referred to communal recitation of a *dhikr*. One of the *wird*s I heard in the *Zawiya* seemed so strange that when I heard scores of *fuqara* rhythmically chanting it, it first made me think of *The Goon Show* and soon I began to seriously doubt my sanity. There could hardly be a mistake. They were all swaying and chanting, 'Yellow teeth. Yellow teeth. Yellow teeth.' But how could yellow teeth inspire such passion among the dervishes? Later in the day I discovered that what I had misheard was actually '*Ya*' (meaning Oh) and '*Latif*', meaning Kindly One, which is one of the ninety-nine names

15. A reunion of the *fuqara* at the *Zawiya*

of God. '*Ya Latif*' was a powerful and subtle *dhikr*. *Dhikr*s and *wird*s are not things for you to have a go at in your own home. One needed the Shaikh's permission to perform the '*Ya Latif*' *dhikr*. The weakest *dhikr* and one that could be recited without permission was '*Istaghfir Allah*' (I beg pardon of God). Usually the *dhikr* was repeated a thousand times and a rosary helped one keep count of where one was in the process. There were two types of rosary – one with three sections of thirty-three beads and another with four sections of twenty-five beads.

One afternoon Harvey and I looked up at the minaret and saw that it had an inscription giving the *hijri* date of its construction (but I cannot now remember what that date was). Anyway, the year 1966 corresponded to the Muslim *hijri* year 1386, only fourteen years short of the Muslim year 1400 therefore, and this led us on to a discussion of Muslim ideas about the End of the World. Harvey suggested to me that perhaps the world had already ended. Only no one had noticed that this was the case. There was a lot of speculation among Algerians that the Apocalypse would take place in the year 1400. 'A sun shall rise in the West and men will wish to believe in it, but they will not be able to.' The erection of high-rise buildings is one of the things that presages the End. According to Muslim tradition, Dajjal, the Muslim equivalent to the Antichrist, will appear on earth in the Last Days. He will be reddish in colour, frizzy-haired and one-eyed. One account says that he will be born in Damascus (and consequently a friend of mine from schooldays, the art critic Peter Fuller, took a perverse pride in the fact he had been born in Damascus). Dajjal will be defeated when Christ appears and his defeat will be followed by the first blast of the trumpet at which all living things will die. But the second blast of the trumpet signals *al-Qiyama*, the Day of Resurrection, and then each person is judged and those who are saved make their away along the bridge over Hell into Paradise. Harvey's and my ponderings on the End of Time need to be seen in the context of the Cold War, the atomic arsenals and MAD (mutually assured destruction).

There were more local traditions. I heard that the Arabs say that at the End there will be only two languages, Arabic and English. The existence of Mostaganem, in the western part of the Islamic world, was in some way held to presage the End of Time. According to Faid, during the last few years of the world the doors to God would be closed to all but a very few – almost nobody in fact. The purpose of the *tariqa* was not to create mystics, but to prepare men for the coming of the *Ruh Allah* (the breath or spirit of God). After 1400 all religion would be finished. Jesus will come, but only in the spirit, not the body, and one had to desert the *tariqa* in order to follow him. The Mahdi (the guided one) would also appear in the Last Days. It might turn out to be the present Shaikh or it might be his son, Khaled, who would be the Mahdi. Khaled, whom we encountered from time to time, was then still a schoolboy, having been born in 1949, but already a great future was prophesied for him. But the Mahdi would probably be someone who was between thirty and forty years old in fourteen years' time. Faid also told me that both the 'Alawi *tariqa* and the End of the World were prophesied in the Book of Isaiah. As it turned out, the *hijri* year 1400, which began in November 1979, commenced with the seizure of the Ka'ba enclosure in Mecca by a self-proclaimed Mahdi, who sought to overthrow the Saudi regime and establish a proper Islamic state, though the Mahdist revolt was swiftly and brutally put down by special forces.

While we were there in the *Zawiya* so many decades ago, Harvey had told me that he thought it possible that one only properly realised oneself as a Sufi in maturity or old age. (This was a notion that Harvey had got from reading the twelfth-century Sufi al-Ghazali on the five stages of man.) That sort of idea matched the message of Hesse's novel *Siddhartha*, in which the youthful hero is possessed by the desire to become a *samana*, a holy man: 'Siddhartha had one single goal – to become empty, to become empty of thirst, desire, dreams, pleasure and sorrow – to let the Self die.' But after three years of fasting and asceticism, he rebels and enters the world of *samsara*, that is to say the everyday world where material values are dominant, and he becomes rich and amuses himself with women. He learns about real life from a courtesan, a rich merchant and a dice player: 'The world had caught him; pleasure, covetousness, idleness and finally also the vice that he had always despised and scorned as the most foolish – acquisitiveness.' Yet all this immersion in the vain and transient proves necessary for the final approach to enlightenment: 'I had to become a fool again in order to find *Atman* in myself. I had to sin in order to live again.' He had been on a spiralling path on which it was necessary to experience the world in order to leave it. Perhaps this sort of zigzag trajectory would be something that Harvey and I would follow and perhaps spiritual fulfilment would be reserved for us in our old age?

> *... to arrive where we started*
> *And know the place for the first time.*
> (T. S. Eliot, 'Little Gidding')

One night Abdullah Faid and another *faqir*, Abdullah Muslim, quarrelled over whether one could walk backwards to God. Abdullah Muslim believed that one could and added that he could see backwards, 'but not very much'. Whereupon Harvey and I got the incipient giggles and hurried from the room and staggered out of the *Zawiya*. In the middle of the street we fell to our knees, howling with laughter, and then I was flat on my face on the street, weeping and convulsed as if by the Demon of Laughter. That daft moment did feel like a kind of exorcism. On another day Faid declared, 'If you laugh at something, that impulse comes from the Devil. But if you just laugh, this comes from God, this laughing without reason.' Again, he once observed, 'The shaikhs, imams and prophets do not laugh. They see so much imperfection in the world, how could they laugh?' and, '*La Tariqa, ce n'est pas un rigolatre.*'

A common Western image of a dervish is of a wild, long-haired figure in rags. But Faid reported that Khaled had said that Harvey and I were still like common people with our scruffy dress and unkempt hair. Why did we not become truly clean and correct? Our long hair in particular was not liked. But Faid said, 'All that will come, when our heart tells us, which will be when God wills.' But we young English-men were so different from the visiting Swiss *fuqara*, who tended to be prosperous businessmen in suits. Meanwhile I was told that I had to comb my long hair and keep it in order. It was an Islamic duty. In those days beards had not yet become a badge of Islamic piety and young men with beards were disapproved of in North Africa, for beards were the prerogative of the old.

On a Friday, a few days before my birthday, I was taken to the main mosque in Mostaganem. There I was brought before the imam of the mosque and I recited the *shahada*, 'I bear witness that there is no God but Allah and I bear witness that Muhammad is his Prophet', in front of him and my conversion was officially registered and duly reported in the local Oranais newspaper. (But I later heard that not everybody approved, for some Algerians believed that Islam was a religion reserved for the Arabs.) Then on the Sunday after the mid-afternoon prayer, there was a large gathering of the *fuqara* in the *Zawiya* presided over by the Shaikh and his *muqaddam*. After the prayers there was an announcement that one of the *fuqara* had become engaged. This was followed by a sermon by the Shaikh and some chanting by the *fuqara*. Then I was led up by Abdullah Faid to repeat the *shahada* three times in front of all the *fuqara*. (A *faqira* – a female *faqir* – who was watching the ceremony from behind a screen later commented that I had pronounced the *shahada* with a strong Oxford accent.) After this, the Shaikh preached another sermon, this time on my conversion. Then the Qur'an was recited, after which the Shaikh told the *fuqara* to recite the *dhikr* 'Ya Latif' a thousand times. A fantastic tension built up among the swaying, straining *fuqara*. Then I and another young *faqir* came up to the Shaikh and offered our hands to him. This was the ceremony of initiation into the *tariqa*. The Shaikh pressed my hand and held it to his chest. Now I was a member, not only of Islam, but also of the '*confrérie*'. An old man sitting at the back of the gathering burst out crying. The chants recommenced and they led into the dance, the '*imara*. This last was performed four times, during which three people went *melboos* (including the dwarf). A short prayer followed and four more people came up to give their hand to the Shaikh. More chants and the dusk prayer followed.

Afterwards I was told by Faid that my Muslim name would be 'Abd al-Rahman, Slave of the Compassionate, a name which I like. A few nights after my conversion, I had a dream in which an aged *faqir* was standing over me and his companion was explaining, 'We do not believe in Islam. What we believe in you will learn later.' (No, I never did, and some dreams are just stupid.)

On Tuesday 23 August Harvey and I celebrated my twentieth birthday at the top of the *Zawiya*'s minaret with some *shema* and a couple of cans of Nestlé condensed milk. We sat up there discussing holy fools, amyl nitrate, the Mahdi, the *Beano*, ritual ablutions and punting in Oxford. We were surrounded by empty and discarded *shema* tins. Taking *shema* in the *Zawiya* was disapproved of, but several of the *fuqara* used to slink off to the top of the minaret for a surreptitious blast of super-strong nicotine – a bit like smoking behind the school bicycle shed. One night I slept at the top of the minaret. It was so cool coming down in the morning, for as I did so I felt as if I was descending into the depths of my subconscious.

This was the summer that I saw the Aissawa and the dancing boys perform. The Aissawa were another order that was just barely tolerated by the authorities. The branch of the Aissawa in Mostaganem was under the protection of the 'Alawis and some evenings they came to sing and perform in the courtyard of the 'Alawi *Zawiya*. By 'perform', I mean that they used to slash their breasts with knives, run spikes through their cheeks, rest hot pokers on their tongues, charm serpents and eat glass. They emerged scatheless through the power of the name of God.

One night I followed the path beside the canyon down to the beach and walked beside the metallically gleaming sea until I came to a kind of folk theatre on the sands. An effeminate youth with a silk scarf slung round his hips

16. An Aissawa snake charmer with a scorpion in his mouth

performed a seductive dance. I walked on into a makeshift chamber where African women with waggling arses were performing what I guessed to be a tribal dance to the sound of metal cymbals. Then the women withdrew to a side of the hall, where they sat screened by clouds of incense. An old black man entered, apparently far gone in some form of possession. He was brought before each member of the orchestra to establish a kind of rapport with them, before he commenced his flagellant's dance and flogged his back with knotted cords. (I think he may have been a member of the Gnaoua, but I don't know. The Gnaoua are a Sufi religious cult comprised of the descendants of slaves of sub-Saharan origin.) I left the hall and the beach and climbed to the top of a cliff, where on the cliff's edge a group of the Aissawa were demonstrating the power of the name of God. Four youths, looking utterly exhausted, clung together in a circle for mutual support. Then they advanced, singing and dancing, towards the drummers. The drummers, seated on the ground, smiled up at them before producing long iron needles each with a heavy metal ball at its end and these they stuck through the tongues and cheeks of the youths. They paraded round the circle of watchers before having the weighted needles withdrawn. Each member of the Aissawa had a special tune which took him into the trance during which he was able to bear his ordeal. But the 'Alawis were amused by this sort of stuff. They regarded it as mere entertainment. There were far more dangerous things on the path of the 'Alawi *tariqa*. Nevertheless, as I say, the Aissawa were friends and allies of the 'Alawis.

According to legend, the founder of the Aissawa order, Ibn Aissa (who died in 1524), was travelling in the desert with a band of forty of his disciples and their provisions were exhausted. 'What shall we eat, Master?' cried the disciples. 'Eat poison!' he replied, pointing to the snakes and scorpions at his feet. Ever since then the Aissawa have practised snake-charming. They also used to take part in a strange ritual called *frissa* in which they used their bare hands to dismember a live sheep.

In his youth al-'Alawi worked as a cobbler, but he also became a disciple of one of the shaikhs of the Aissawa, an order which, besides practising the sort of self-mutilation I had witnessed, also practised fire-eating and snake-charming. Although he became proficient in these practices, he eventually drifted away from them, except for keeping his hand in with snake-charming. One day he was visited by a certain Shaikh Buzidi, who asked al-'Alawi to show him how he handled snakes and al-'Alawi obliged, but when he had finished, the Shaikh asked if he could not charm a snake bigger than the one which he held in his hand and continued, 'I will show you one that is bigger than this and far more venomous and if you can take hold of it you are a real sage. I mean your soul, which is between the two sides of your body,' he explained. 'Its poison is more deadly than a snake's, and if you can take hold of it and do what you please with it, you are, as I have said, a sage indeed.' (The word Buzidi used for soul here was *nafs*, which refers to the lower soul and is to be distinguished from the *ruh*, the breath or higher soul.)

When al-'Alawi took the hand of Shaikh Buzidi, a shaikh of a more mainstream Sufi order, and so became his disciple, al-'Alawi had attached himself to a *silsila* that ran all the way back to 'Ali and the Prophet Muhammad. Al-'Alawi had received an initiation from a shaikh of the Darqawi order and, going many generations back, a Darqawi shaikh had received an initiation from a shaikh of the Shadhili order and, so link by link, the chain of transmission could be traced back to the origins of Islam. When Buzidi died in 1914, al-'Alawi, who had been his disciple for sixteen years, founded his own order. Then the Aissawa wanted to join it, but they found that they could not take its spiritual power, which was too strong for them. The 'Alawiya followed a highly orthodox version of Sufism in which all the obligations of Islam were observed. Al-'Alawi went on to have a leading role in reviving orthodox Islam and presenting it to a mostly North African audience as intellectually and spiritually respectable – indeed admirable. He impressed European visitors by his Christ-like appearance, as well as his excellent French.

The *Zawiya* was under a kind of double siege. One was conducted by the politico-military apparatus of Algiers and their henchmen in Mostaganem. But there was also an invisible siege mounted by Iblis, the Devil, and invisible jinn. Good jinn who had allied with the Shaikh were the driving force in the *Zawiya*. A *faqira* told me that one should not allow dust to accumulate in a room as the jinn used that dust to form themselves and thus evil might be engendered by dirt. I asked Abdullah Faid about the jinn. Faid recalled that, when he was a young sailor, he was on the same ship as a Buddhist navigator who had to work hard to drive the jinn out of the ship's engine room – this as a prelude to a homily about the jinn in the *Zawiya*. Certain jinn were the driving force in the *Zawiya* – good jinn who had allied themselves with the Shaikh. Until Jesus was thirty, no one knew anything of him. But, when he received his revelation, the people who opposed him could see a jinni. Jinn are spiritual projections of the *nafs*. Jinn were visible in the *Zawiya*. If one has a jinni, it means that one has not expanded enough. I asked Faid what the jinn were. He replied that they were projections of the *nafs*. Confusingly, the lovers of God acquired the most jinn. When I asked Faid why Hell existed, he just laughed silently. I walked out fuming.

The Shaikh had a lot of trouble from the jinn, but he used the Qur'an and, even more, the *'imara* to free his disciples from them. It is because of the jinn that many of the *fuqara* are afraid to perform the *'imara*. Years ago some *fuqara* had driven out into the countryside and past a certain house.

They were invited in and they were regally entertained with food and song and given beds for the night. But when they awoke the following morning the house had vanished. It had been a mirage conjured up by benevolent Sufi jinn.

I learned all sorts of stuff which was not really part of Islam, but which was really local custom or just superstition. For example, you should not point your feet at people you like, or at Mecca, or at the tombs of the Shaikhs. I had a recipe from Sidi Abdullah Muslim for getting rid of a headache: take a fistful of salt and hold it to the side of the head for ten minutes and recite from the Qur'an. After ten minutes throw the salt away for it has drawn out the evil. There was a slight prejudice against even numbers. God, after all, was one. It was better to do a thing three times rather than twice. In Arab folklore, if one dealt a jinni a good blow with a sword, then he was killed, but if one was foolish enough to strike him again, he came back alive. Wild gestures were disapproved of, for this was not part of the etiquette of the *Zawiya*.

Whistling was disliked. According to the Qur'an, women whistled upon knots to create spells. Whistling seemed somehow to be associated with *waswas*, the whispering of evil suggestions. In the Qur'an, *Sura* 114, *al-Nas* (People), runs as follows:

In the name of God the Merciful, the Compassionate

Say: 'I take refuge with the Lord of men,
The king of men
The god of men
From the evil of the slinking whisperer in the breasts of men
Of jinn and men.'

According to commentators on the Qur'an, 'the slinking whisperer' is Iblis, who whispers doubts into men's minds.

Waswas was held to be the cause of much of the rancour in the *Zawiya*. I was aware that there were factions who were contending for the approval of the Shaikh, though, since I was a visiting foreigner, I did not understand what was at stake between those factions. But the point is that, as in any enclosed community, ancient feuds were fought out and there was a lot of jostling for power. In that respect the *Zawiya* was just like an Oxford college.

My esoteric tutorials with Faid continued. He was unable to stop preaching and he talked and talked even if those around him could not understand a word that he was saying. His talking, he claimed, was just something that happened to him without his willing it. A *majdhub* could say things that the Shaikh dare not, but the *majdhub* has drawn those things from the Shaikh. He spoke often of Shaikh Hadj Adda, the previous Shaikh who had given him his initiation and sent him into *khalwa*. The first and the third Shaikhs were hard men and hated as such, but Hadj Adda was soft. He had to be, for his task was to hold the *tariqa* together. He had started out as al-'Alawi's chauffeur. He was married five times and divorced four times. Shaikh Hajj Adda once declared that there were three kinds of *fuqara* – lions, monkeys and pigs. The lions fought the shaikh, the monkeys put on an act and the pigs ate everything that was put before them. The *fuqara* were a great trial to the current Shaikh – Shaikh al-Mehdi. Abdullah Faid told me that the *fuqara* who stayed all the time in the *Zawiya* were no more than the jinn of the shaikhs. But, of course, Abdullah Faid was one of those *fuqara* himself. The teachings of the order were pervaded by paradoxes, such as 'Beauty is the veil of the Beautiful' or 'He who is closest to God is furthest from Him', or the medieval Sufi al-Ghazali's saying that 'Paradise is full of blockheads.' Such observations or maxims were known as *mudha-karat*. More generally there was a stark and paradoxical

116

ambivalence at the heart of the practices of the *tariqa*. There was a lot of talk about the outer forms of Islam and of all religions being worthless, and even as constituting an obstacle on the path, but yet there was strict observation of those outer forms, prayers, ablutions, fasting and all the rest of it.

Faid claimed that Jesus and Muhammad were socialists, but they were not like the socialists of today, whose socialism was all '*Moi, moi, moi.*' (That was a very fair comment on the sort of socialism that was practised in Algeria in the sixties.) Faid always stressed obedience to the Shaikh. Nothing mattered more than obedience to the Shaikh. Faid despised what he called *ahl al-kitab* (people of the book), people who had turned to worshipping the Qur'an, rather than God. When he spoke about Sufism and Islam more generally, he not only spoke sense, but was inspiring. But sometimes his words were more crazy than holy. It was a mistake to let him get on to talking about the Druids. According to him, the Druids had a lineage that could be traced to the Biblical Abraham (and, by the way, the Indian God Brahman should be identified with the Abraham of the Bible and the Ibrahim of the Qur'an). So the Druids of Brittany constituted a branch of the religion of Abraham and their white robes were a sign of their purity.

Like my Oxford tutors, Faid thought that I had promise. At one point he told me that I might become a shaikh, *in sha Allah*, and on another occasion he told me that I was so restrained and complicated that I might become another Schuon. (Well, at least I have avoided that fate, I think.) Faid also said to Harvey, '*Ça va avec Sidi 'Abd al-Rahman. Son spirit marche vite. Il est malade avec l'amour.*'

There is an erotic component to mysticism. Here, in Martin Lings's rather archaic translation, is the opening of a poem by al-'Alawi:

Full near I came unto where dwelleth
Lailā, when I heard her call.
That voice, would I might ever hear it!
She favoured me, and drew me to her,
Took me in, into her precinct,
With discourse intimate addressed me.
She sat me by her, then came closer,
Raised the cloak that hid her from me,
Made me marvel to distraction,
Bewildered me with all her beauty.

The woman's name, Lailā, or Layla, also means 'Night' and Lings notes that here it is to be understood as representing the Divine Essence. Similar mystical imagery can be found in the Christian mystical tradition. For example, take these lines from 'Songs of the soul in rapture at having arrived at the height of perfection which is union with God by the road of spiritual negation' by St John of the Cross (in Roy Campbell's translation):

Oh night that was my guide!
Oh darkness dearer than the morning's pride.
Oh night that joined the lover
To the beloved bride
Transfiguring them each into the other.

So in the darkness I would lie awake and I waited to be ravished by the Unseen, but I trembled, for surely intercourse with the Infinite would be a terrible thing? God knows, I was not ready for such an encounter. According to the medieval mystic Meister Eckhart, 'If man is to become fruitful, he must become a woman before God.' A union between God and man implies the total annihilation of the man's ego (or, in Arabic, his *nafs*). It is a strange business believing that one is in love with the Invisible, particularly when one is young. It was, perhaps, like falling in love with a girl whom one has never seen, but only heard of by report. But when I thought about it then, the mystic union between man and God was horrific and obscene, like copulation between a man and a shark. Sometimes God was a shark, sometimes an electric fist, sometimes a beautiful woman, sometimes the Arabic letters of his name, sometimes a great void and sometimes a black sun sending out pulsations in spheres of light. It was better not to think about these things.

By the way, 'Layla' is also the title of one of the most famous love songs in the history of rock music. It was released by Eric Clapton in 1970 and it commemorated his then unrequited love for Patti Boyd. On this famous recording Clapton declares that he is on his knees before Layla and there is a quite wonderful intensity to his repeated incantation of her name. The lyrics are based upon the medieval Arab story about the love of Qays ibn Mullawah for Layla. Qays went mad from unrequited love and consequently was renamed Majnun. As Majnun he lived in the desert with the wild beasts. Sufis have customarily interpreted this story as an allegory of love for the Divine and, as it happens, Clapton was told the story of Layla and Majnun by a friend of his, Ian Dallas, who had recently converted to Islam and joined the Darqawi *tariqa*.

Sidi Abdullah Muslim once sarcastically remarked of Abdullah Faid, 'Sidi Abdullah is not Sidi Allah.' Even so, he respected him enormously. When Hadj Adda was Shaikh, everyone had to undergo the *khalwa* and they reached God through it, as had Abdullah Faid. That was why Abdullah Muslim respected Faid so much, because he had been in the *khalwa*, whereas Abdullah Muslim had not. But *khalwa* had been discontinued. Faid told me that before he had entered *khalwa*, he had taken the Shaikh's hand and thereafter throughout this period of spiritual isolation it felt as though the Shaikh was there with him. But when he emerged from *khalwa*, the Shaikh was gone. 'In *khalwa* you are likely to see demons, but they are from within you. In *khalwa* the veil over your heart is removed and you can see the devils there, but when they are expelled, the veil returns over the heart and you can no longer see inside.' Also he cryptically observed that the *fuqara* used to compare the *khalwa* of al-'Alawi to a cinema show.

Apart from Faid, Abdullah Muslim was the *faqir* who talked to me most. He told me that the *fuqara* had no sense of property and that if they took something it was not stealing, for anything in the *Zawiya* was theirs. He thought that it was impossible to concentrate in the *Zawiya*. He used to be very good at concentrating on his work, but not any more, for his heart sent him this way and that and he could not even concentrate on crime novels any more. Previously he had been attached to the Darqawi *tariqa* and that had been a very different thing. According to Abdullah Muslim, Harvey's second visit to the *Zawiya* was harder for him than his first and each year it would become yet more difficult.

The Shaikh el-Mehdi had a brother who hardly ever spoke, but, while Harvey was there that summer, he suddenly started to speak and continued for three days discoursing on holy things, hardly stopping at all. Just before the brother had started to speak, Harvey had seen a blinding flash of light come from him.

All things are perishing before His face.
He who loves me, him I love. He whom I love I kill.

It was said that in the *Zawiya*, he who wished to preserve his personality would lose it and he who wished to lose his personality would gain it. That may well have been true in my case. I had very little personality when I arrived there and what little I had I tried to lose, but, without wishing it, I ended up with more of me than when I started. I was very intense and perhaps projected that intensity on the place that I was in. In a dream a *faqira* reproached me with being '*trop chaud*'. At times, during the hot nights looking up at the minaret under the stars, I had thought I was in Paradise. I was very hot – in both senses of the word – and absolutely determined to become someone's disciple and to learn from someone else how to be. Yet I was in turmoil, for how could I possibly know that I was approaching God and not the Devil? How could I know that I was not dying to the Devil? And I was often ill – feverish or ravaged by toothache. Sometimes I was homesick and missing things like salad, cigars and literary magazines. Mostaganem was fly-blown, sweaty and a bit boring. When one sets out on a mystical path one anticipates all sorts of horrendous obstacles, but not boredom. Yet boredom there must be. Mostaganem was a strange place in which to try to grow up.

At the end of that summer in Mostaganem I got a lift from a *faqir* who was going to Oran. As he drove, he played a tape recording of Anne Lindgren saying the *shahada* on the day of her conversion. After she recited the *shahada*, she continued, 'My dear brothers, I don't know what to say', and then she could be heard weeping. In Oran I stayed at the 'Alawi *Zawiya* in the Rue des Ouled Nails. That evening there was a big reunion and a procession along a cliff top. Then there was an unusually fierce dance in which the heads of the *fuqara* almost swept the ground.

My passage across the Mediterranean was unproblematic, but hitching through France proved difficult and drivers roared past me as if I were an ornamental plastic roadside gnome.

Back in England that autumn I was a walking flame. I was possessed by a horrible energy, but going nowhere. I did not expect to live for very long. As a line from the Who song put it, 'I hope I die before I get old.' Fired up by

Surrealist and mystical writings, I tried to imagine all sorts of strange things, but I just could not imagine getting old. In the autumn of 1966 it seemed to me that I had no destiny, for my future was blank. Now, as I write, it seems to me that my destiny is already mostly in the past.

Islamic doctrines about fate and predestination are quite dour and even dull. Centuries before the universe came into being, everything that shall happen was written on *al-Lawh al-Mahfuz*, the Preserved Tablet, for Allah knows in advance everything that we shall do. Kismet (fate) is the Turkish form of the Arabic word *qisma*. Kismet has entered the English language, though it is more the sort of word that turns up in novels, particularly old-fashioned ones. Kismet is a pattern imposed on the lives of his characters by their Creator. A character in a novel may behave as if he or she has free choice, but that is not the reality, for his or her actions are determined by the creator, the novelist. It may appear that Tess of the d'Urbervilles has been sentenced by a jury to be hanged for murder, but the reality is that it was Thomas Hardy who decreed her death. It is most probable that she was already doomed even before he put pen to paper. It may well be that the universe we inhabit is like that and that our sense of being free to will what we do next is merely an illusion.

I spent a few uneasy days in Chobham with my parents before the Oxford Michaelmas term. The profession of religion and more specifically the act of prayer outside their normal cultural context can seem strange. In the Surrey hills, in the midst of the stockbroker belt, home and family, I would prostrate myself before the Ruler of Jinn and men and the Judge of the Fiery Pit whose fuel is men and stones.

In the autumn term of this year, Zaehner, having lectured on the Vedanta in the previous year, resumed his lectures on Sufism. This time I was not his entire audience, for the room was full of young men with long hair and beards and young women in jeans or flowery miniskirts. By now Sufism was in vogue and I guess that many of those present had been reading Idries Shah's popular book *The Sufis*. Zaehner looked round with bafflement and suspicion at his new audience, many of whom were sitting cross-legged on the floor of his study. In the years to come he developed a strong antipathy to hippies. In *Drugs, Mysticism and Make-believe* (1973) he denounced the idea that drug-taking could lead to enlightenment and he attacked the Californisation of Oriental religions in the West. As for hippies, 'They make themselves ridiculous because they are trying to do what can only be done without trying. Try to be spontaneous and you will only succeed in becoming conventionally unconventional.'

Later, *In Our Savage God: The Perverse Use of Eastern Thought* (published in 1974, which was also the year of his death), he produced a strange and confusing meditation on the murder of Sharon Tate and her companions in 1969 by Charles Manson and his followers. Invoking the Upanishads, the Vedanta, Rimbaud and the Catholic novelist Georges Bernanos, Zaehner tried to put the slaughter in a mystical context. In the course of this rambling book, he suggested that it was boredom that was fuelling youthful revolt and driving them to follow Eastern gurus. He also fingered the Satanist Aleister Crowley as the man who introduced Indian sex magic to the West. Also I guess that Zaehner was getting back at the unwashed hippy students who dared intrude upon his rooms in All Souls back in the sixties.

I started my special subject, which was on 'The Scientific Idea in the Seventeenth Century'. This was an interesting and important subject, but what interested me in it was its occult penumbra: John Dee's spirit raising, Newton's alchemy, Kepler's mystical and astrological preoccupations, Joseph Glanvill's writing on mesmerism, as well as

K.BRADFORD D.ROGERS R.FREEDMAN R.IRWIN

MERTON · OXFORD

17. *University Challenge*, 1965. Though there were complaints about our long hair, mine was to grow longer yet

Glanvill's and Robert Boyle's interest in demonology. In the summer I was part of the Merton team on *University Challenge*. The advance briefing discouraged us from wearing white shirts or black jackets. We were trounced in the quiz and afterwards people wrote in to complain about our long hair, but a trio of girls in Belfast wrote to me to say they really fancied me.

According to Proust's *Contre Sainte-Beuve*, 'La Rochefoucauld said that only our first loves are involuntary.' But are they not all involuntary? Late in the November of that year I met a nurse on a blind date. Here I shall call her Juliet. After Juliet and I met in London and had dinner, she came up to see me in Oxford the following day. For both of us it was unplanned and unexpected. We listened to Ravi Shankar and the Beatles in my room and later we walked hand in hand round Christ Church Meadow. Afterwards, I took her round to see John Aiken. That afternoon he confidently lectured us on the crystal memory banks that were concealed in Peru, Persia, Tibet and elsewhere; the impossibility of building pyramids today; mystic union conceived of as existence at the sub-atomic level; the end of the Brahmin *Kalpa*; prophecies by Jehovah's Witnesses regarding the End of the World; the Kundalini yoga system and erotic heresy in Oxford; what higher mathematics could tell us about the End of the World; the architectural codes of pre-Inca civilisation; the hypnotic basis of Indian mysticism; Sufism as black magic; black magic to be considered as white magic at the highest level; evidence for the lost continent of Lemuria; how civilisations flourished on top of electromagnetic fissures; marriage as a way of making dialectical progress on a spiritual path. John always smiled as he poured this stuff out. He was a walking encyclopedia of dodgy knowledge. What was I thinking of, exposing Juliet to all this?

She was very pretty and had been offered work as a model. Though she was not a classical beauty, I thought that she looked like Jean Shrimpton. She had long brown hair and a pleasantly curvy body. I thought then that she was the most marvellous person I had ever encountered in my life. I thought that, if it meant risking eternal damnation for her sake, so be it, but of course I kept that sort of thought to myself and, for the time being, I kept quiet about Islam and the *Zawiya*. While I tried to conceal the raging neurotic beast within me, she was soft and kind. She wanted to live in a cottage in the countryside with roses climbing up the walls. She enjoyed teasing me. She used 'Super!' a lot. Trouser suits alternated with miniskirts. She liked skiing, riding, cooking, sailing, amateur dramatics and expensive meals. She shopped for pleasure and I enjoyed watching her array herself. Virginia Woolf's *To the Lighthouse* had made a great impression on her. She wanted to be like Mrs Ramsay. She kept saying, 'You don't know me. You just don't know what I am like', and eventually she was to prove to me that she was right about that. But, come to think of it, she did not know me either. For a while, I was successful in impersonating a normal, healthy person. She lodged in a nurses' hostel in Victoria and all her friends there seemed to be continually in one kind of emotional crisis or another. Later, when I came to read Muriel Spark's *The Girls of Slender Means*, I thought that I recognised that place.

She came to Oxford some weekends and I went down to London as many weekends as I could manage (or more, and consequently my essays and seminar presentations suffered). We used to walk hand in hand down the King's Road. In those days it was not monopolised by the same chain stores and coffee houses one sees in every part of the country now. Then there was Mary Quant, Granny Takes a Trip, the Chelsea Drugstore and Gandalf's Garden and, just off King's Road, there was Hung on You. Just as important, there were still local grocers and cobblers, as well as second-hand bookshops and antiques stalls. By now, the logic of commerce has destroyed almost all of this and no one in their right mind would bother to walk the length of King's Road for pleasure. But then: 'In Chelsea, the girls in their breathtaking short skirts, their outrageous dresses inspired by anything from *art nouveau* to the Union Jack, their mad stockings and kinky boots, their obvious acceptance of the stares of stunned, gasping males, are so tantalising and so beautiful that any account of entertainment in London must inevitably give them pride of place' (Milton Shulman).

Juliet and I also went to Bunjies Coffee House and Folk Cellar just off Charing Cross Road, for she was keen on folk music, but it took me decades to catch up with her on this. We went ice skating on the Queensway rink, which in those days was a decorous place and, halfway through the session, ordinary skaters had to clear the ice for performers of the foxtrot, the tango and the paso doble. We went to films. She annoyed me by preferring Rupert Birkin to Gerald Crich in Ken Russell's *Women in Love*. (I had iden-tified with Gerald and I had a flicker of a sense that her preference for Rupert might not be good news.) We saw the film version of the Royal Ballet production of *Romeo and Juliet*, danced by Fonteyn and Nureyev and choreographed by Kenneth Macmillan. Of course, the power of the music was enhanced by being in love and, contrariwise, pop lyrics helped one to articulate one's emotions. The Incredible String Band, the Monkees and Donovan helped guide my feelings.

In Oxford I took her punting. On one occasion she lost a shoe and I carried her back to college in my arms. I also introduced her to more of my friends, a few of whom were relatively normal. It was difficult to see much of her, for she was often on night duty or on weekend duty and I had seminars and tutorials that I had to attend. When she was on night duty she started letters, long letters that straddled over several days. In the early letters she often wrote about her ideal in life being to curl up on a rug in front of a fire with a hot drink and a good book in some safe suburban place. (In the sixties, by the way, people still wrote letters frequently and at length.) I became her reading counsellor and got her to read Thomas Mann and other heavyweight novelists, but she still read medical stuff like *The Sea Within: The Story of Our Body Fluids* by William D. Snively. But, in later letters, the cosy domestic theme faded somewhat and there was a lot more of a sense of her inhabiting a swinging London. She was writing to me about fast cars, fast-talking people and quick changes of clothes. By now human love and divine love were mixed up in my mind.

18. Adam and Eve

5

THE SUMMER OF 1967

FOR MANY PEOPLE of my generation the summer of '67 was special. For me personally it was a disaster. It is actually painful to read my diaries for that year. There is so much passion and despair in them. Wild thoughts about love, friendship, society, patterns of history and God all exploded in my head. I took a long time to recover from this year of loss and failure.

This was also the year that two former leaders of the Algerian War of Independence were murdered on the instructions of the Sécurité Militaire. Mohammed Khidr was assassinated in Madrid in January and Krim Belkacem was strangled in Frankfurt in October. The second murder seems to have been carried out by one of the FLN's leading thugs, a man known as Vespa. (I will have occasion to come back to Vespa later in the book.) What's more, I did not go to Algeria in 1967. Donovan's 'Mellow Yellow' was released in January. I spent much of that month reading St Thomas Aquinas. According to Aquinas, 'In a sense, we can say of God that he is made of nothing, since he is not made at all.' Also, less predictably: 'Scratching done without attention is not, properly speaking, a human act.' The Beatles's 'Strawberry Fields' and 'Penny Lane' came out in February. The reference in 'Penny Lane' to 'the pretty nurse' who was selling poppies always makes me think of Juliet. More generally, both sides of that Beatles record in their melancholy way celebrated normality and the small pleasures of provincial life.

By now, the sixties (in the sense of colourful clothes, long hair, drugs, tarot cards, the youth cult and the rest of it) were in full flood. 'If you were there in the sixties and can remember it, then you weren't there' is merely glib. How could any of us who were there (Alzheimer's sufferers apart) forget the sixties? Kaleidoscopic light shows, dancing in the nude, stoned laughter, silvery dresses and a lot of frivolity. According to Roland Barthes, 'Tinsel is better than gold. It has all the qualities gold has, plus pathos', and Barthes was echoed by the sixties photographer David Bailey, whose *Box of Pin-Ups* declared, 'David Bailey is fascinated by tinsel – a bright, brittle quality, the more appealing because it tarnishes so soon.' We had our own language, the *Lingua Orbis Sexaginta*: verbs – score, grok, rap, goofing off, sass, faze, ball (as in ball a chick); nouns – joint, roach, spiff, stash, smack, head, raver, teeny-bopper, roadie, high, fuzz, buzz, vibe, drag, bust; adjectives and phrases – cool, spaced out, uptight, groovy.

Yeats wrote of:

The Land of Faery
Where nobody gets old and godly and grave.

But the trappings of the sixties gave warnings of their transience. One was supposed to wear flowers in one's hair, the image of the butterfly was everywhere and a lot of bubbles were blown. The psychedelic moment was only a moment and it was obvious that it could not last. But while that was going on, the other, respectable England and the comfortable certainties that I had known as a child were also passing away. Margaret Thatcher declared in 1982,

'Fashionable theories and permissive claptrap set the scene for a society in which old values of discipline and restraint were denigrated.' Perhaps this is right, but Thatcherism also played a part in the destruction of Old England. The country inns turned into gastro-pubs or something worse. The corner stores and specialist shops, owned by and staffed by identifiable individuals, were giving way to big commercial chains. Brown paper bags were replaced by plastic bags. The countryside was first marked out as Green Belt and then, having been so designated, became the target for property developers. People ceased to form orderly queues at bus stops. On the buses I no longer received Victorian pennies in my change. In cinemas people no longer stood for the National Anthem before the main feature. Englishness and pride in being English were downgraded in favour of 'cultural diversity'. (But this has turned out to be a one-sided transaction. There is no cultural diversity in Saudi Arabia.)

The wartime feature films and documentaries made by Michael Powell, Emeric Pressburger and Humphrey Jennings had celebrated an England that, as it turned out, was left mostly untouched by the bombing of the Luftwaffe, but which was destroyed subsequently by the politicians and property developers. Though there is no point in me going into a reactionary rant about the England we have lost, I feel wistful about my memories of the Surrey countryside that I used to roam across and I have the absurd belief that the clouds and the blue skies looked different then. *Tempora mutantur et nos mutamur in illis.* Looking at Orientalist paintings, the nineteenth-century romantic novelist and essayist Théophile Gautier claimed to feel nostalgic for the desert, even though he had never been in one. In a similar fashion, I feel nostalgic about Britain in the Second World War, even though I was not born then. With a pang I recognise places, people and hardships. It is absurd, but there it is.

By now I was in my final year and the approach towards Finals. History remained interesting, but it was not as interesting as God or women. I worked fitfully and revised incompetently. I have a poor memory. The great historian Sir Lewis Namier said something to the effect that ignorance is a powerful tool for the historian, as it helps sift out indigestible and superfluous information. He may have been right, but having a poor memory is not really an asset when it comes to taking exams. Also, I kept taking days off to go to see Juliet in London or welcome her to Oxford. At a London party we danced to Alan Price's 'Simon Smith and His Amazing Dancing Bear'. Then, a little later, she came up and put her hands over my shoulders, pinning me to the wall, and, looking deep into my eyes, said, 'I love you.' In Oxford, I took her punting again. Kneeling on my chest, her eyes covered by her long dark hair, she lectured me. 'Don't put me on a pedestal,' she said. 'There is a lot you don't know about me.' True, and her message was already familiar. Apart from anything else, I did not know who else she was seeing, but I had a sense that other men circled her like predatory sharks. These men were mostly slightly older, much more mature and they were talented musicians or great skiers, or both. They also had money and drove fast cars.

Towards the end of the previous autumn term, I had got into trouble for being associated with drug takers. The college decreed that I should be gated and, since it was no longer possible to visit Juliet in London when term recommenced, I had to explain to her why. She, who was wonderfully straight, was shocked. By now she was also aware that I was a Muslim and a Sufi. Things were becoming more difficult.

In the spring, in April I think, Sidi Hajj Madani visited Oxford on a kind of mission from Mostaganem. He was prospecting the possibility of setting up a *zawiya* in England

132

(and I think he had also been instructed to see what we young English *fuqara* were up to). Not knowing what else to do with him, I took him to the cinema to see *A Man for All Seasons*. He had no English, so I had to do a whispery translation of all the dialogue into French. The film about the life and death of Sir Thomas More meant nothing to him. He had not come to England to waste his time going to the cinema. He was shocked by the prevalence of drug-taking in Oxford and other signs of hedonism. Drugs were bad for the memory, he told me. Though by then he was a fierce puritan and devoted *faqir*, he had had a colourful past. At one stage he had run a strip club, after which he had been a policeman in Algiers under the French, before switching his loyalty to the FLN. Despite his background as a heavy, he had got to know Louis Massignon, the famous Orientalist, and Frithjof Schuon, the proponent of the Primordial Tradition. He warned me against having anything to with the followers of Gurdjieff. (It was a warning that I did not heed.)

After declaring that Oxford was not yet ripe for the *tariqa*, Madani left in an ill humour, for he saw that everybody was rushing around expending their energy in futile ways and he told me that I understood nothing about Sufism and should not meditate. There was only misery in Sufism. It did not matter whether I ate pork or not. He said that I should force the Shaikh to give me guidance and he also told me that I should marry. In the meantime, I should fix myself up regularly with a prostitute! While he was in Oxford, he met Juliet and could see that she was unhappy, but he thought that she would make a good wife.

Juliet had mysterious fits of crying. In the late spring we walked through a Surrey wood and stopped on a little wooden bridge over a stagnant stream. Her head rested on my shoulder. After a long silence, she began to talk about death. I had never ever felt so strongly that I was a character in a novel. Later she cried when I told her that I wanted to marry her. I told her that I would leave God and the *Zawiya* and drop all my crazy ideas to be with her. Had not Faid told me repeatedly that one should go where one's heart told one to go? But still she remained scared of my religion.

The summer of '67 was very summery. In the TV series *The Prisoner*, the men paraded around in boaters and blazers and the women carried parasols. It was like that in Oxford too. As Nick Cohn put it: 'Hippie was largely a summer sport. Bare feet and silks and universal brotherhoods – these things were not created for an English January.' The sun was celebrated in Donovan's 'A Sunny Day', 'The Sun is a Very Magic Fellow', 'Sunny South Kensington', 'Sunshine Superman' and 'Writer in the Sun'. The summer's beauty gave an edge to what was going to happen.

In March one of the great rock albums of all time was released, *The Velvet Underground and Nico*, the vinyl embodiment of nihilistic New York cool. The lazy, lush, lulling cadences of the opening track, 'Sunday Morning', are deceptive, for they deal with paranoia. But other tracks have urgent driving rhythms and deal with the drug experience. The pounding attack of 'I'm Waiting for the Man' is about the desperate need for a fix and the lyrics of 'Run, Run, Run' are also about scoring. 'Heroin', with its slow build-ups to the fast-tempo highs and then slowed rhythms, is more about coming down than it is about getting high. And there is a lot of sex, delivered in the Snow Queen Nico's breathy 'Femme Fatale' and the gentle lyricism of 'I'll Be Your Mirror', as well as the excruciatingly harsh sounds of 'Venus in Furs', with its conjuration 'shiny boots of leather'. Then there was the melancholia of 'All Tomorrow's Parties'. *The Velvet Underground and Nico* presented the sounds of dark enchantment and carried a curse. The group did not last long. Nico left after this album was released and, having become a heroin addict, died young. So did Edie Sedgwick, the original 'Femme Fatale'. Someone remarked of the Velvet Underground, 'If it wasn't for bad luck, they wouldn't have no luck at all.'

In June the Beatles released *Sgt. Pepper's Lonely Hearts Club Band*. It was the anthem of 1967. In Oxford colleges it was played over and over again and we searched the lyrics for hidden meanings. Beneath all the brassy oompah, there was an undertone of sadness to that record. The innocent joy of Alan Price's 'Simon Smith and His Amazing Dancing Bear' and the Monkees' 'I'm a Believer' gave way to sadder lyrics. The elegiac sound of Procul Harum's 'A Whiter Shade of Pale' caught the mood of that season and Juliet wrote to me about its captivating melancholy. In general, it is striking how many of the pop lyrics were set in the future and looked back to the present from a position of defeat and compromise. The Beatles merely wondered what it would be like to be sixty-four, but Donovan in 'Hi, It's Been a Long Time' presents himself as re-encountering his former girlfriend (she was looking fine) and giving her a lift in his flash car. Similarly, the Incredible String Band's 'First Girl I Loved' looked back on first love at the age of seventeen and speculated that that girl was by now probably married and with children. It was as if regrets were being stockpiled for the future and this lyrical theme was echoed in visual terms by David Bailey's photographic compilation *Goodbye Baby & Amen: A Saraband for the Sixties*. Defeat, the sell-out to maturity and 'the toad work' were almost universally anticipated by the lyricists. It was also anticipated that the first love would not last. Even so, as the *International Times* put it sometime in 1967, 'If our ideas are squashed in the future we can look back on the ball we had now.' I did have a ball, but a sad one.

I invited Juliet to Pembroke College's May Ball, also known as the Eights Week Ball. (Whatever Eights Week means – something to do with rowing, I think.) It was in late May. The psychedelic rock group the Who had been hired to play for the first hours of the night, which were designated for dancing. They played music from *A Quick One* and what, later that year, would come out as *The Who Sell Out*. Lyrics such as 'My Generation' were ostentatiously rebellious and 'Pictures of Lily' was an ode to the joys of masturbation, but the Who's audience that night consisted of swells in dinner jackets and debs in ball gowns, all grooving in a starchy sort of way. At the end of the Who's act, coloured smoke filled the marquee.

Woody Allen once observed that if he could have his life all over again, he would not bother going to see the film version of John Fowles's *The Magus*. I would, for it is not that bad a film. But, if I had my life all over again, I would go to dancing lessons when young. Perhaps the greatest regret of my life is that as a schoolboy I had resisted my mother's pressure to go to dancing classes with those disturbing creatures known to Nigel Molesworth as 'gurrls'. I had failed to anticipate how important dancing would become in the sixties. At the Pembroke ball and later, at venues like Middle Earth and UFO, I twisted and wriggled uneasily, never really sure whether what I was doing counted as dancing. But at the ball I successfully faked it. It was a warm summer night and, dinner-jacketed, with a beautiful and affectionate girl beside me and tipped by my tutors to get a first in the fast-approaching Finals, I should have been on top of the world, but yet I had a sense that things were not right.

After the ball, I had to work, to revise hard. It was not possible to get down to London and Juliet sounded vague on the telephone. For Finals, which started at the beginning of June, subfusc – dark formal clothes worn in combination

19. The Merton historians celebrating the end of Finals. Our history tutor Dr John Roberts looks on as I pour champagne into David Jessel's glass

with the academic gown – was obligatory. The young women in white blouses, black skirts and dark stockings were distractingly desirable. There were, I think, three papers on 'The Scientific Idea in the Seventeenth Century'. It had not crossed my mind that my future examiners might not share my interest in the occult roots of the scientific movement and I struggled with the questions they actually asked. The history papers were crammed into little over a week and they coincided with the Six Day War. I remember taking tea with another Merton historian, John David, who was Jewish, and I listened to him debate with himself whether to walk out of Finals and go to Israel to serve the country in this great emergency. (In those days most people in Britain thought of Israel as a gallant little democracy menaced with extinction by the mighty armies of the Arab world.)

After Finals finished I spent three days in bed reading that over-size ramblers' manual *The Lord of the Rings*. A little after Finals, on the night of 14 June, I had a dream in which I was at a party and everyone at the party wore weird masks, including Juliet. Then suddenly I realised that I was not with her at all. 'You didn't really think that it was her, did you?' the horrible masked thing mocked. I woke with relief from the nightmare, and thought that I was blessed, for it was only a nightmare and the real Juliet was coming up to Oxford to see me that day. But the nightmare spoke the truth. She arrived in Oxford on a painful mission. On a punt on the Cherwell, she told me that she was seeing someone else and that she was leaving me. I could not stop crying. She said that she did not actually love this other man, but it was a fatal attraction and that she felt like a fish on a hook. I saw her back to the station and then wept again all the way back to college.

We continued to correspond and to see one another occasionally. She was suspicious of my sudden decision to come to London to do postgraduate studies (to be near her of course). And how long did I intend to remain a student? And how would the world benefit from my studying Arabic? (Good question.) On one occasion, she turned on me and said, 'People might sit around talking about doing sensational things, but where is the reality in that? You need to get to know yourself and recognise your limitations.' She also fretted about my frequent fits of depression.

Breaking up with Juliet was difficult and, as it turned out, I was always to be bad at breaking up with women.

I brooded and I wrote long argumentative letters, as if one could win a person's love by force of debate. In one break-up after another, the woman would want us to stay friends, but friendship was not what I needed. I had plenty of friends, albeit weird ones mostly. I needed love and emotional reassurance and it was too painful to face relegation to just a confidant and a recipient of letters, from then on enjoined to look at but never to touch the adored one. It is sad that I spurned the friendships that I was offered and, in retrospect, I am ashamed of it, but that was how it was. I am ashamed of it even now. I wanted never to see Juliet again. No, I wanted to see her once more to fix her in my memory, but then never again. I needed to explain to her why we should never meet again, or, alternatively, why I had changed my mind about that. It was not a clean break. We did have a series of meetings that usually turned into sullen rows. But in the very long run, as Walter Savage Landor had it, 'There is no name, with whatever emphasis of passionate love repeated, of which the echo is not faint at last.' Then the religious madman in me demanded to know how, if I could not worship a sweet young girl as she deserved to be worshipped, could I worship God?

On the subject of breaking up, a year or two earlier a friend in Magdalen had told me how he found out that he had been betrayed by his girl after he saw another man's car outside her house. He wandered the streets of Oxford and when he was stopped by the police and asked which college he was from, all he could say was, 'I am sad. I am sad.' He explained his (Jungian) notion that when a man loved a woman, he transferred his anima, his feminine side, to the girl and the girl reciprocated by transferring her male aspect to the man. Hence the pain and jealousy when a woman betrayed a man, for she took the man's anima away to be raped by another man.

After Juliet I lost even more weight. These days I am a

substantial figure and it seems incredible now, but I became so thin that I could put my two thumbs and forefingers round my waist. A few years later I was part of an encounter group where we all had to strip naked. The only person who could think of anything nice to say about me was a woman who said that I had the body of a flamenco dancer and that 'from an artist's point of view I had a superb rib structure'.

> *Odi et amo: quare id faciam, fortasse requiris,*
> *Nescio, sed fieri sentio et excrucior.*
> (I hate and I love. You may ask why I do so.
> I do not know, but I feel it and am in torment.)
>
> (Catullus)

And according to the thirteenth-century Sufi Jalal al-Din Rumi, 'Love is a torture. Love kills.' On the other hand, Bertrand Russell remarked, 'I think people who are unhappy are always proud of being so, and therefore do not like to be told that there is nothing grand about their unhappiness.' But for me then unhappiness seemed like a good idea. It was the right answer to being betrayed and dumped.

Demented by grief, for a while I even managed to forget my Christian name. Driven crazy by my loss, Majnun should have been my name. Medieval Arab medical treatises discussed love as a form of madness, for love burns the brain. '*Ishq* is the Arabic word for excessive, passionate love. According to the tenth-century physician, philosopher and alchemist al-Razi, one should wean oneself away from seeing the beloved and remember that ultimately death separates all lovers. At one point it crossed my mind that I had invented Juliet. Maybe she never existed and perhaps my friends had been humouring me and my invisible 'girl'. I never found it easy to sleep after the break-up. The ticking of a watch or the slither of a raindrop down a windowpane would keep me awake.

In retrospect, I am surprised that Juliet had stuck with me for as long as she did. I was so full of third-rate, amateur metaphysics and poorly understood mysticism. I was boringly intense, hideously needy and apparently without any idea of what I was going to do with my life, never mind what would have been our hypothetical life together. Meanwhile, there were plenty of more mature men with jobs, money and a sane outlook on life out there. What to do? I thought a lot about suicide. I had read so much Dostoevsky that I was well up on suicide. I brooded in my room surrounded by drug manuals, LPs out of their sleeves, unanswered correspondence, guttered candles, empty *shema* tins and unwashed coffee cups. The curtains were closed as I clawed back obsessively over the past. I replayed Donovan's music and now I heard that its promises of sunshine, prettiness and lace were all false. In my mind he had become a sinister Pied Piper leading the flower children on to destruction.

Towards the end of the Six Day War I walked in on my grandfather (a passionate admirer of General Franco), who was watching on television the Israeli tanks pursuing fleeing Egyptians. He turned to me with a cackle: 'I never had much time for the Yids, but look what a hiding they're giving to the wogs!' That war and the shock of the Israeli victory meant that it would be dangerous to go to Algeria that summer. The whole Arab world was enraged by British and American support for Israel. The truth was that negligence, corruption and incompetence had doomed the Arab armies, but Nasser's regime had put out lying propaganda that the RAF had fought on the side of the Israelis and that at least one of the British planes had been shot down on Egyptian soil. My brother, who happened to be on holiday in Egypt that summer, was stoned by a mob, taken into police custody for his protection, then released only to be rearrested and interrogated as a spy by military intelligence. Finally, with other British people who had been rounded up, he was deported to Cyprus. If I remember rightly, a Russian cruise ship came to collect him and other deportees. Algeria had declared war against Israel and broken off diplomatic relations with the United States. Inside Algeria synagogues were first defaced by angry mobs and then confiscated by the state. The few Jews who had remained in the country after independence were driven out.

A few weeks before Finals began I had spotted something on the noticeboard in college. It read as follows:

Something must be done to relieve the desperate plight of families living in overcrowded, inferior and highly rented accommodation ... to meet some of those needs we are organising a summer project ... both the housing and the play projects are being used as a focus for community organising. This summer people living in Notting Hill will be encouraged to organise themselves into community groups, in order that work started can be continued ... it is a challenging task ... we cannot do it alone. Therefore we are appealing for 200 students to join us and make the summer project successful. Can you resist the call for help?

What possessed me to respond to this? Perhaps it was an attempt to get to know other, more ordinary people? Perhaps my reading of Danilo Dolci's impassioned accounts of poverty in Sicily had ignited a latent idealism? But I think that what mostly lay behind my volunteering somewhat resembled that scene in old-fashioned novels where the young gentleman, who has been accused of cheating at bezique, or of being a coward, and consequently has lost the love of the woman he had hoped to marry, goes into the Foreign Legion in order to forget. (Think *Under Two Flags*, or *The Four Feathers*, or *Beau Geste*.)

The Notting Hill Summer Project Community Workshop was conceived of against a background of the race riots of the fifties and the Rachmanism of the sixties. Rachmanism has entered the English language. As the *Chambers Dictionary* has it: 'Rachmanism ... the conduct of a landlord who charges extortionate rents for property in which very bad slum conditions prevail.' Peter Rachman specialised in acquiring rented property and then using violence or subterfuge to drive out the sitting tenants, who were mostly white, and then he replaced them with mostly West Indian immigrants who were forced to pay extortionate rents. Up to the day of his death in 1962, he got away with it and it was only the outbreak of the Profumo scandal in the following year that led to the exposure of the extent of his racketeering, for it so happened that both Christine Keeler and Mandy Rice-Davies had been his mistress. At the time of its exposure in 1963, Rachman's slum empire was estimated to be worth £18 million. Though he was no longer around, his heirs and lieutenants still held sway in the area. 'Michael X' was a particularly sinister enforcer who later fled to Trinidad, where he was found to have murdered Joseph Skerritt and Gale Benson.

Anyway, in the summer of 1967 the Notting Hill People's Association instituted a survey of the Colville and Golborne slum areas of North Kensington. Why are young people idealistic? There were approximately a hundred of us students who had each paid £8 for the privilege of working on the housing survey and lesser parallel projects. I see from his autobiography, *Hitch-22*, that Christopher Hitchens was one of the volunteers, though I do not remember him. His book evokes the racial mix in the area: 'Padding around Notting Hill was an education in cheek-by-jowlery. Spicy Indian restaurants along Westbourne Grove, the West Indians and their ganja funk around the Mangrove in All Saints: Irish pubs where the regulars were

not entirely thrilled by the arrival of the latest immigrants.'
The prostitutes were mostly white, but their ponces were
almost all West Indian. (Ponce is a sixties word which seems
to have since dropped out of circulation.)

George Clark, of the Community Workshop and a well-
known CND campaigner, was in charge of the project. In
an opening address, he told us that it was not a clear vision
of the future for this area that drove him, but sheer anger.
He was also fearful of the possibility that we volunteers
might say or do the wrong thing and so spark off a new
race riot. A lot of the volunteers were sociology students
or trainee social workers. There were some CND veterans,
a few anarchists and more Trotskyists. In the early days,
before the structure of the survey had been properly ham-
mered out, we had plenty of time for talk and most of the
talk was argument. We sat on the pavements under the July
sun and some of us swigged from little brown bottles of
Dr J. Collis Browne's Chlorodyne, a patent medicine with
a long history of soothing the ill-defined complaints of
old people. Available at most chemists, it was alleged to
contain cocaine in small quantities and it certainly offered
a gentle high. One had to swig the whole bottle and it
tasted foul, though not as foul as opium tea, which I came
to later.

We argued about politics mostly, but also about music,
linguistics and art. Occasionally religion cropped up and
here I found it difficult to defend my position coherently.
The answer I formulated at the time was that in order to
understand Sufism you have to become a Sufi. It is impossible to understand it from the outside. At Mostaganem I had
found a doorway through which I could enter upon a living
mystical tradition and a high-level esoteric path. I claimed
that I had brainwashed myself into believing in Islam. But
the best reason for believing in Islam is because it is true
and Paradise awaits the believer. Although the above does

not really make sense, it was what I was saying at the time. While we waited to go into action, we learned how to make badges with slogans on them. Mine were as follows: 'The Mahdi Comes', 'Rebuild the Koranic State'; '*Non Civitas Terrestris sed Civitas Psychedelitas (sic)*'; '*L'Amour, la Mort, Une Chose*'; 'Opium for the Religion of the People'. We slept in sleeping bags on the floor of a school and later we were moved to a church. When we rose from between the pews in the mornings it was like a painting of the Resurrection by Stanley Spencer. Eggs were boiled for breakfast in a school dustbin. One evening a gang of us went to see Yoko Ono's mind-numbingly tedious film *No. 4*, which featured a sequence of bottoms. (Yoko Ono features in my list of ghastly iconic sixties people. Others in the list are Franz Fanon, Richard Neville, Richard Harris, Herbert Marcuse, David Hemmings, R. D. Laing, Frank Sinatra and Simon Dee.)

Once the survey proper got under way I became closely acquainted with poverty and fear. Though I had actually seen worse poverty in Algeria, in Notting Hill I saw a lot of smashed banisters, broken windows and mattresses soaked in urine. Where there were lifts, they had been used as public toilets. In this sort of context how does a piety like 'God is within you' help? In Algeria there was a lot of poverty, but not this sort of squalor. (In ancient Egypt, by the way, poverty was regarded as a disease.) I interviewed a lot of unmarried mothers. One member of my team interviewed a woman with fourteen children. Another woman was offering her daughters to the landlord as payment of the rent. Multiple levels of subletting led to wild overcrowding. Loud music blasted out of clubs in cellars.

The terror in this part of west London was pervasive. The tenants I spoke to feared intimidation, eviction, rent hikes and even visitors from the social services. We were feared as snoopers from the council or some other menacing official body. I had a local man as a bodyguard for some of my visits. Occasionally the tenants were afraid of less tangible things. One afternoon I was working my way along a cul-de-sac called Ruston Place with my clipboard and questionnaire about living conditions and rents when I came to number 11. A West Indian woman admitted me to her dark basement flat. There was no electricity and, as we talked in low voices in the shadows, we strayed off the questionnaire a bit, as she told me that she and her children had to use the outside lavatory in the garden of number 10, but her children were afraid to because of the corpses that had been buried there and the ghosts that rose from its soil at night. Ruston Place had been known as Rillington Place until 1953, when the bodies of John Christie's victims were found there. He had buried two in the garden. Three more women were stored in the kitchen alcove behind some wallpaper and his wife, Ethel, was buried under the floorboards of the kitchen. Although the woman I interviewed was black, the man she was living with would have supported the fascist British National Front, only he had got the impression that their leader was a 'bloody foreigner'.

The area was densely populated and becoming more so. The Westway was under construction at that time. The trendy clothes shop I Was Lord Kitchener's Valet was at 293 Portobello Road. Hippies had started to move into the area and it was becoming a druggy scene. The Mangrove, a Trinidadian restaurant on All Saints Road, was the place to score, or, failing that, the Finches, a pub on Portobello Road. Apart from hash and Methedrine, there was a foul-tasting thing called cola nut, which, once digested, would keep one going for thirty-six hours.

In the end the survey interviewed 5,000 households. According to the Rent Act of 1965, every tenant was entitled to a rent book and this was one of the things that we

20. Me in my silver shirt from Carnaby Street in the summer of '67. I am high on I cannot remember what

were supposed to check on. Since it was strictly a set questionnaire, I might find myself asking a mother of five living with her family in two rooms, 'Do you make full use of these rooms?' 'You're joking of course.' The real purpose of the survey was to turn people on and to create a sense of community, but in this I think we failed and the neighbourhood remained unmobilised.

New play sites opened up in Notting Hill. Since it had not been a clean break with Juliet, she came to see me once and spent a day helping me run a street playground just off Portobello Road. She was a heart-stopping vision as she stood, tenderly maternal, in the midst of a crowd of infants (a bit like Snow White with the seven dwarfs). There were occasional breaks from the squalor of this part of Notting Hill, for a short walk took me down to Chelsea and the King's Road and its boutiques and memories of better times with Juliet. That August I listened to the London Philharmonic playing Dvorak's *New World Symphony* in Holland Park and it felt like a refresher course in what it was like to be middle class.

On 29 July I got news of my second-class degree (and not a particularly good second class). Despite the best efforts of my tutors, I still had an ill-disciplined mind. Also, having started off lonely in my first year, by the second year I had too many friends. Almost every evening they had continued to troop into my room (which was conveniently situated in central Oxford) and talk about tantric sex, the Vietnam War, Situationism, adrenalin highs, the pros and cons of suicide, Marshall McLuhan, the Catholic doctrine on masturbation, hyperspace, the Cabala, *The Savage Mind* and so on. I should have been with other, duller people and talking about the Golden Bull of Charles V and Gladstone's fiscal policy. And then there was mysticism. And then there were drugs. And then there was Juliet.

I developed an inferiority complex about my second-class degree. Throughout my early years at school I had been relegated to the C stream (and hence was assigned carpentry, rather than Greek or German, and it was not even as though I had any aptitude for carpentry). Now I was branded for ever as having a second-class mind. This was the background to my application to join Mensa. Having passed the first IQ test, which one did at home, I went on to the LSE, I think, to sit the invigilated second test A few weeks later I learned that I had passed that one too, but while I had been sitting that, I had taken a close look at my fellow examinees and decided that I did not want to have anything to do with them and so I never did join Mensa. A little later, however, driven by the same inferiority complex, I took up the *Times* crossword. A month after I got my degree result, the Notting Hill Summer Project Community Workshop ended.

I briefly revisited Oxford. Sometime in the autumn I went for the day because another English *faqir*, who had been given the name of 'Abd al-Qadir, had recently returned from Mostaganem. He had news of various kinds. Faid had been banned from the mosque for disturbing the prayers. The Shaikh was concerned about the health of all us English *fuqara*. The *fuqara* in Mostaganem were planning to establish centres in Europe and hold street marches with everybody in green robes with red hearts painted upon them. Flying saucers were suddenly popular in Oxford and 'Abd al-Qadir was one of several of my friends who claimed to have seen one, though inevitably it was John Aiken who was the real expert on flying saucers and the men in black. (A visitation by the men in black was at least as disturbing as the sighting of a flying saucer. These men, slight and dark-skinned and wearing black suits or pullovers and wraparound sunglasses, would turn up to interview and threaten anyone who reported seeing a flying saucer.) While I was up in Oxford, a gypsy in Cattlemarket told my fortune. I would be closely connected to a hot country, travel to many foreign lands and write a book which would make me a lot of money. I was an unusual person, out of the common run, and I lived on my nerves. (It was that obvious.)

Though I could not travel to Mostaganem, it was around this time that I encountered a kind of literary Doppelgänger of Abdullah Faid, for Maggi Lidchi's novel *Earthman* was published this year. In it the English protagonist travels to Ceylon and India, where he ends up in an ashram as the disciple of a red-haired Irishman, 'the Irish Swami'. The Swami bombards his new disciple with paradoxical formulations and impossible demands. Complete obedience was required. As I read it, I thought that the similarities to what I had experienced in Mostaganem were downright eerie and I wondered if Lidchi had actually been to Mostaganem and was writing about it in an Indian guise. Having looked at the book again for the purpose of writing this,

I am less impressed with the parallelisms. Early on in the novel, the Englishman becomes obsessed with keeping a diary, but then the Swami burns it: 'Irish Swami said that it was a crutch and that all crutches must be destroyed.' Faid never demanded that my diary should be destroyed, though perhaps it would have been better for me and for him if it had.

I had registered to do research in Middle Eastern history at London University's School of Oriental and African Studies in Bloomsbury. It was a crowded, scruffy place. It is much larger now, but still crowded and scruffy. Bernard Lewis was my designated thesis supervisor. Although he was already quite well known as a spokesman for Israel and Zionism, he had yet to become the counsellor of the Neo-Cons in the United States and to popularise the expression 'clash of civilisations'. His advocacy of the pre-emptive bombing of Iranian nuclear installations was some way in the future. But I had no idea how grand this man already was. He was yet another in a long sequence of teachers. Like Zaehner, he had been a spy during the war, but he never talked about it.

Since he was an eloquent, witty and lucid speaker, the lecture room was usually full with students from all over London when he spoke. He was a literary stylist and he produced sensitive and passionate translations of poems from Arabic, Turkish, Persian and Hebrew. A collection of these translations, *Music of a Distant Drum*, is arguably his best and most revealing book, though in those days his best-known works were *The Arabs in History* and *The Origins of Modern Turkey*. He had mastered Hebrew, Aramaic, Arabic, Latin, Greek, Persian and Turkish, as well as, of course, French, German and Italian, and, I think, Russian. Later, a former colleague of his told me that Lewis said that he had acquired a reading knowledge of Arabic, Persian and Turkish in two terms and he found it difficult to understand how anyone could spend a year studying just one language and still not be fluent in it. He certainly found my slowness in getting to grips with medieval Arabic incomprehensible. But, eventually, he agreed that my proposed M.Phil. could be upgraded to be registered for a Ph.D. Its title was something like 'The Mamluk Reconquista: The Muslim Reconquest of the Crusader States in the Late Thirteenth Century'. Since neither he nor I had much interest in talking about this, most of the supervisions were spent discussing Marxism, Freudianism, Jungianism and the Cold War. Lewis would reminisce about the year he spent as a research student of the mystical Orientalist Louis Massignon, as well as his attempts at Orientalist conferences to lure Russian academics away from their minders.

If I was going to become a historian of the Middle East, then the key language I had to master was German. Lewis was adamant about this and he dispatched me to a special course at University College on German for archaeologists. Since I was already having difficulty with Arabic, this extra load was not welcome. The decision to study Arabic had been over-determined as a necessary part of my researches into Middle Eastern history. I thought that it might be interesting to find out what the medieval Arabs thought of the Crusaders. Then I wanted to get outside my skull and no longer have my thinking constrained by the limits of twentieth-century English. I wished, through the newly mastered language, to have a different sense of time, space and identity. I thought that if I studied thirteenth-century Arabic and absorbed that language as my own, then I might learn to think like a thirteenth-century Arab. Also, of course, I was studying God's language, the language in which He chose to speak to humanity in the seventh century AD.

Arabic was more difficult than I had anticipated. The

letters changed shape according to where they were in the word and whether they were joined to the letters in front of them and behind them. Since the vowels were not usually written out, one had to guess them. There were forms, called broken plurals, in which the inside of the noun changed drastically. There was a special noun form for colours and undesirable physical characteristics. There were consonants that had no equivalents in English. Punctuation was absent in pre-modern texts. The layout of words in Arabic–English dictionaries was not a simple alphabetic one, but was organised by (usually) trilateral roots and in my early days with this language I could easily spend half an hour with Wehr's Arabic dictionary as I tried to guess the root of a particular word. A large number of words have at least two meanings, one of which is likely to be the opposite of the first. And then there are many problems with numbers. For example, as Professor Beeston observed, 'The substantive numerals 3–10 have the odd feature that they exhibit the "feminine" marker when the numbered entity is masculine in the singular, and are not so marked when it is feminine …' There is an old saying, 'Only a prophet is able to have perfect command of the Arabic language.' It was while I was immersed in the study of Arabic that I had a dream that I was learning the *walawala* language instead. It was incredibly simple, as it just consisted in saying *walawala* over and over again. Sadly, the language I was actually learning was not like that.

In the autumn I had moved into Roupell Street, an attractive street of little houses close by Waterloo Station that were, I believe, built originally for railway workers. Thereby I fell in with a rather wonderful community of young people, spread among two or three houses in the street. There was a strong artistic component to this community, which included a sculptor, a book illustrator, a jewellery designer, a potter, a trainee artist, a trainee actress and a book-binder, but also a nurse, a classics student, a Ph.D. student in anthropology and a town planner. Besides the young artists, an older generation of circus folk had settled in the street and a pair of retired acrobats ran the corner shop. People came and went and moved from house to house and there was a lot of bed-hopping. It was difficult to be lonely in Roupell Street, but sometimes I managed it.

I had a tiny room, not much larger than a stair cupboard, for which I paid one pound and ten shillings a week. Most of the space was taken up by a bed and the house's water tank. The room had bare white walls. In bed at night I used to press my cheek against it to feel its chilly dampness. One night there was tapping on the wall. I sat up in bed. 'Are you a poltergeist?' I asked. 'Tap once for yes and twice for no.' There was just the one tap. Beside the almost invari-ably rumpled bed, on the little table, were two rosaries (one Muslim and one Christian), a book or two, some recent correspondence, an ashtray and some Italian fermented cigars. Later, I added a Japanese Buddhist rosary. On a lower shelf, I kept a card index amateurishly devoted to symbolic imagery, an Arabic–English dictionary and more cigars. Books, magazines and newspapers were piled on the floor, which was filthy. I worked at my Arabic and slept in a haze of dust. I used to spend hours observing the damp patches and cracks on the walls and I tried to form images out of them (as Leonardo da Vinci urged us to do). On one wall there was a picture of a magician. On another there was a picture of a film actress in black leather. The curtains were almost always closed. When open, the view was of a brick wall. It was a cell for a hermit. I used to 'hear' silent voices in my head. There was so little floor space that it was difficult for me to do the Islamic prayer.

I looked back on what, in retrospect, had become golden

days in Oxford. I sat cross-legged on the bed and scribbled *pensées* in my notebooks. I watched the dust drifting across the room and thought about the jinn who might be inhabiting that dust. The first autumn was melancholy, for I felt myself to be mediocre, and why not? I had done nothing much so far. I was also intensely bored. When was something going to happen in my life? In the meantime I was considering writing a novel about one of the walls of my tiny room. Nothing would happen in this novel, which would nevertheless be acclaimed as a tour de force of monomaniacal, concentrated observation.

I learned to live on sliced white bread, macrobiotic brown rice, Brussels sprouts, boiled eggs and bars of chocolate. It was a bit of a comedown after the years of gracious living in Oxford. Lunches at SOAS were cheap and tasted it. Since the bathroom in 46 Roupell Street was freezing cold, I usually took baths at the University of London Union. Lice turned up in some of the beds in number 46. Lambeth Council sent an expert on vermin control and, sucking through his teeth, he described with relish the life-cycle of the louse and how it can survive for years in the walls by cannibalistically feasting on its brethren. There were no lice in my tiny room. I persuaded myself that it was the cigar smoke that killed them off.

I composed what I called an 'Archaeopsychic Map of London'. Its spine ran from SOAS, representing the brain, down Charing Cross Road towards Waterloo. The headquarters of a cult known as the Process and Watkins occult bookshop featured on it. So did various places that were the sites of meetings with or separations from girlfriends. Roupell Street was the groin.

I was a little unusual in that I lived in an upstairs room, for these were the basement years and most of my friends from Oxford seemed to have found dark, subterranean lodgings in various parts of Notting Hill (and mostly they found

jobs in the incipient profession of computer programming).
Unlike my first year in Oxford, I was not lonely in London.
Even at first I met all sorts of strange and beautiful people. I
had friends but ... Kevin Jackson, in an illuminating discussion of that great sixties film *Withnail and I*, gets it right:
'It feelingly portrays the intensity and insecurity of adolescent friendships – are *these* the people I am going to be
stuck with for the rest of my life? – the dread of loneliness,
directionlessness and humiliating, total failure in "the terrible years in your twenties".' I did not want nice friends. I
wanted interesting ones. None of my contemporaries had
televisions and this was still the age of letter-writing. I kept
getting demanding and genially abusive letters from Peter
Fuller – 'shit face' was a typical term of affection – wanting
me to come and see him in Cambridge, wanting me to come
out and join him on Mount Athos, wanting me to accompany him to India.

I was supposed to be researching the history of medieval
Egypt and Syria, but I actually spent more time researching who I was and who I might become. Why was I doing
research? I think that, in the beginning, it was merely a way
of postponing deciding what I wanted to do and actually
signing up for a job of work. Though I had no ambition
to become an academic, I wanted to read and think for
some years longer. A day or two after enrolling at SOAS, I
wandered into Rafiq Bulent's Oriental bookshop and conversation with its proprietor led on to an introduction to
a junior representative of a secretive Ouspenskyite Study
Group. He met me outside the London Planetarium and,
as we walked through Regent's Park on a bright clear day,
he cross-questioned me about my background and the seri-
ousness of my motives. As he did so, I began to get some
notion of the people he represented, who were mostly smart
and wealthy. In the sixties esotericism was popular among
members of the upper class.

After this vetting, I was vetted again by Dr Rolles, a former disciple of Ouspensky, before I was permitted to attend a Mevlevi dervish ritual performed by Westerners somewhere in the Barons Court area. The origins of Mevlevi dervishes go back to thirteenth-century Konya in Anatolia and the teachings of Jalal al-Din Rumi. Mevlevi music is slow and beautiful and the dance ceremonious. Its performers wear tall conical felt hats and black coats which are cast off during the ritual to reveal white garments underneath. The dancers turn quite slowly, their arms outstretched, with the right hand turned up to heaven and the left hand turned down to earth. Both the music and the whirling dance are heavily laden with symbolism, relating to death and resurrection and the planets circling the sun. As with the 'Alawi dance, there is someone who moves among the dancers checking their performance, but in other respects the Mevlevi dance is very different from the 'imara. It does not feature the terrifying acceleration of tempo that is characteristic of the 'Alawi dance. The Mevlevis' movements are more pleasing aesthetically. But I felt no *baraka* and my heart did not ignite. In the twenties Kemal Atatürk banned all Sufi orders. Although in recent years the Mevlevi dance has been revived in Konya, it is for the tourists. Members of the real Mevlevi *tariqa* are in exile in Syria and Cyprus.

By the way, I later met Rafiq Bulent's brother, Ali Bulent, an antiques dealer, who described himself as an Uwaysi Sufi, as he had been initiated in a dream by Khidr. Uwaysis are dervishes who have not received an initiation from a human master. Ali Bulent taught Reshad Feild, who became a well-known figure in British Sufism and the author of *The Last Barrier: A Sufi Journey*. Ali married a sister of King Farouq.

Now that I was in London, investigating secretive spiritual and occult groups became my hobby. (I think that, as much as anything else, I needed to have an interesting enough life to write about in my diary. I blame my diary.) That summer I made several visits to the headquarters of the Process at 2 Balfour Place in Mayfair. The Beatles record *Revolver* was playing over and over again in the all-night coffee bar known as Satan's Cave. Adherents of the cult in long black capes and wearing silver crosses drifted in and out. They had an air of certainty and superiority. It was an interesting place to get a cheap light dinner. The speciality was corn-on-the-cob. But one evening I took a friend, Chris Brockway, there and after we had finished our corn-on-the-cob a black-robed attractive blonde waitress came to our table. 'Would you like some cake? Are you sure you won't have some cake?' This seemingly neutral proposition from the waitress seemed to Chris to have a triple tier of reference. On the one hand, she might just have been persuading him to have some cake. On the other hand, this might have been a way of getting to know her, a sexual thing then. (Chris was very good-looking.) But perhaps not everything was at it seemed and it might be that this agent of Process was manoeuvring him to accept a bit of cake as the preliminary to luring him into the nefarious toils of the Process. Chris refused the cake, mostly because of the third consideration, but also because I was not having cake. I hate cake, but I did want to see if he would accept a slice of cake as the first stage of getting on with the girl. What fun we had in those days.

Though the men had long hair and beards, these were trimmed and groomed. The cult, headed by Robert and Mary DeGrimston, attracted smart young professionals. Adherents had to dedicate themselves to one of three ways, that of Jehovah, Lucifer or Satan. But the big thing was not to be identified with the 'Grey Force' of 'hypocritical compromise and respectable conformity'. They also had to hand over their wages, all but one pound a week, to the

Process. They claimed that it was as if they were on a permanent LSD trip. From talking with them, I gathered that they, like the Scientologists, from whom they had broken away, were trying to break down people's psychological defence mechanisms and then use the consequent excess energy to develop telepathy and other psychic powers. They did psychic exercises such as gazing into people's eyes for prolonged periods of time. Or they would pair off with another person to spend five minutes attacking that person, followed by five minutes of compliments. This sort of thing anticipated the imminent arrival of encounter groups. I took part in a session of the Telepathy Developing Circle which lasted an hour and twenty minutes, during which we sat on the floor in a candlelit room. We were supposed to develop psychic powers through brief spells of meditation.

Later, I attended a black mass there 'based on the performance of the Beast', meaning the performance of Aleister Crowley. A lot of Crowley's terrible poetry was read out early on. We sat around the stairwell looking down on what was enacted below. The main part of the ritual was like something out of the film version of Dennis Wheatley's *The Devil Rides Out* and it was aesthetically rather pleasing, as it featured black and gold robes, a dark vessel containing a mysterious black potion, a silver mirror, black candles and *The Book of the Law*. The robed celebrants were the Deacon, the Priest, the Virgin Priestess and two long-haired acolytes. The Priestess wore white, the men black. The high point was when the Priestess was stripped down to her underwear and made to lie spread-eagled on the altar, where she was kissed all over by the Priest. There were no dark manifestations and I heard someone mutter that the Priestess was not really a virgin. It was not Satanism, but merely theatre. It was about this time that Peter Fuller went back to visit our old school. 'How are the

Irwin brothers?' our former housemaster ('the Gnome') enquired. 'Irwin major has become a practising Satanist and Irwin minor is a frog in a pantomime' was the reply. 'Oh.'

Out of the sunshine and lurking in the shadows the ghost of Aleister Crowley was one of the presiding spirits of the sixties. He was particularly popular then because of his advocacy of drug-taking and his antinomian 'do what thou wilt shall be whole of the law'. You can see him lined up with the rest of the Beatles pantheon on the sleeve of *Sgt. Pepper*. There he is on the back row, sandwiched between the guru Sri Yukestawar and Mae West. Soon after *Sgt. Pepper* came out, the Rolling Stones released *Their Satanic Majesties Request*. (Never mind that it had a naff sleeve showing them pretending to be wizards, having apparently robed themselves from a child's dressing-up box. The music was pretty naff too.) The group Led Zeppelin bought Crowley's former house in Scotland. Graham Bond was another musician who was into Satanism. In the end he threw himself under a tube train in 1974. It is easy to assume that the underground magazine *Oz* derived its name from the fact that Australians like Richard Neville had set it up. But, according to Crowley, Oz means magic acting on the world of matter. *Rosemary's Baby* and *The Devil Rides Out*, both films about Satanism, were released in 1967. Kenneth Anger's extraordinary *The Inauguration of the Pleasure Dome* had come out the year before. Jayne Mansfield, who belonged to the LaVey Church of Satan, was killed in a car crash in 1967. Also in 1967 Alex Sanders, self-proclaimed King of the Witches, was living in Clarincade Gardens in Notting Hill. I had read a lot of Crowley. What he wrote was interesting, but it was undercut by a marked streak of vulgarity – something which was also a feature of Wheatley's fictions.

I attended classes at the School of Economic Science.

Though their posters in the tube stations advertised courses on philosophy, what one actually got was sub-occult tripe derived from Ouspensky. I also got to know Tony Hutt, another student of Arabic at SOAS. He was attached to the School of Economic Science and used to disappear frequently to meditate. It was probably because of his long-standing membership of the School that he had lots of seriously wealthy friends, though he was not rich, having squandered a family fortune on an art gallery which had failed. But he still had a beautiful flat, whose living room featured a pagan mural of fauns and satyrs that had been executed in charcoal one night by a drunk Catholic priest. The place was decorated with prints and drawings by Braque, Picasso and Cocteau, as well as Persian carpets and a Mamluk bronze candlestick. During his time in Egypt he had had all his grotty Penguin paperbacks rebound in gold-tooled leather. He played records of Tibetan and Mevlevi music and he introduced me to the hits of Diana Ross and the Supremes. British esotericism in the sixties was dominated by the upper class and the lower class hardly got a look in.

Tony had been to a party for which Richard Todd and Elizabeth Taylor had taken over Battersea Funfair. Though it had rained on the day, every guest had been given an umbrella. On 2 December Ben Wint and I went to Battersea Funfair, but it had just closed for ever. The gay decorations now looked tacky and guard dogs patrolled the high-wired perimeter. I turned to Ben. 'This is what your sense of humour looks like when you are not using it.' It was a freezing, grey day and I was just starting to observe Ramadan. Since the Muslim calendar is lunar, Ramadan slowly moves through all the seasons of the solar year. One starts the fast when it is light enough to distinguish a white thread from a black one and one finishes the day's fasting at nightfall. The good thing about Ramadan in a northern winter was that the fasting period was quite short. Even so, I felt the cold and it was difficult to concentrate and work for an Arabic exam. Once I blacked out in a bookshop. Also it was awkward to be observing Ramadan in a house full of non-Muslims.

Shortly after Christmas I went up to Leeds to participate in a Muslim student conference at the university. The conference took place during the last three days of Ramadan. It was cold and the skies were grey. In all respects the conference was a decidedly bleak experience, days of fasting, prayer, sermons and pious discourse. I had so little in common with my Muslim brothers. They had not read Rilke or Hesse and they were not interested in Surrealism. So part of me wished that I had not read those books either and that I had never heard of Surrealism. I was fascinated by the campus of the university. If only I had not gone to Oxford I might have been happy here (as indeed my daughter was to be happy at Leeds a few decades later). Ramadan is no fun, but within Muslim society it does perform the valuable function of reminding the rich what it is like to be poor and hungry. Also, of course, it concentrates one's mind on one's religion. (On another matter, I had had no problem in abstaining from alcohol, since I did not like the taste very much, nor, come to that, did I have the money.)

The day after my return from Leeds I met Peter Fuller, who, for his part, was on the lam from his strict Baptist parents in Bournemouth. Incoherent with relief, we crowded into my tiny room and he threw out his arms and declared that he was 'like an apostate Christ who has decided that he is not going to let himself be crucified after all'. We lit up Italian fermented cigars and jabbered at one another. After the jabber was temporarily exhausted, we visited several casinos, where Peter lost money and we unsuccessfully looked for a prostitute. How we can have been so unsuccessful in the heart of Soho I can no longer remember. We did find a strip show featuring 'The Astounding Spider Woman', but real spiders dancing might have been more sexy. (We both fancied ourselves as intellectuals, but if Aldous Huxley was right that 'an intellectual is someone who has found something more interesting than sex to think about', then neither Peter nor I had got past first base.)

After Soho, we headed off into the night towards Cable Street to look for an opium den that someone at Oxford had told me of. In those days the street was very slummy and infested by consumers of cider, mandrax and hashish. We entered a barber shop (but why?) and discovered that the hairdresser was none other than the Himalayan Swami Ananda, founder of the new Global Religion and dispenser of mantras to anyone who would pay. He told us that, if we bought one of them, within seven days we would perceive the Blue Diamond within ourselves. He showed us letters from satisfied customers who wrote in to confirm that they were now bathed in flashing lights (but I thought that it would probably be better for everybody if they used soap and water). The Swami told us that religion was for children. Peter told him that he would consider becoming his disciple. We moved on to a nearby pub and watched hashish being traded at the bar. We did not find the opium den. It is one of the sadnesses of my life that I have never found an opium den. Later we returned to a Soho casino in an attempt to recoup our losses, before returning to Roupell Street to carry on discussing sex, poetry, the Meaning of Life, a masturbation machine, auto-crucifixion and the utter impossibility of total sincerity.

At Epsom College we had been the top intellectuals and, as such, both friends and rivals. He was a year younger than me and he went up to Peterhouse in Cambridge the year after I went to Oxford. He claimed to be haunted by demons and produced numerous pictures of them, some of which I still have. Like me, he enjoyed (or suffered?) the faculty of hypnagogic imagery and perhaps his demons appeared in those visions. When he was not busy insulting someone, he tended to speak in a slow, low monotone. He told me that he was parodying language by speaking so slowly. I did not get it then and I still don't. In his college, being noisily abusive and clever, he was taken up by one of the most famous dons of that generation, the right-wing political historian Maurice Cowling. Peter once took me to dinner with Cowling. The other guests included Peter's sybaritic cousin George, the well-known historian John Vincent, an aspirant undergraduate poet from Bolton called Mike Haslam and John Parkes, who was a disciple of the inspirational Catholic chaplain of Cambridge, Father Gilbey. I remember the cigars and port circulating, but, alas, have no memory of the conversation. (Damn it.) At about the time I was dropped by Juliet, Peter was dropped by Jenny. Cowling then told Fuller that there was no answer to love thwarted except intense suffering for at least six months and when this was relayed to me I derived cold comfort from it.

Eventually, Peter joined me in London, where he got a job with the *City Press* after telling the interviewers that he had a first in economics from Cambridge, though, if I remember rightly, it was actually a third in English. He made himself supremo of the arts page and I used to accompany him to the openings of plays. Quite often we would walk out during the first interval, since he had already seen enough to write a stinker of a review. Peter and I used to meet in the Macabre Coffee House in Soho. Its tables were shaped like coffins and there were skulls everywhere. The jukebox featured such popular numbers as 'The Ride of the Valkyries'. He was undergoing psychoanalysis to cure himself of the addiction to gambling, something that had started in the bookmaker's close to the Epsom racecourse.

Of course, betting had been a beatable offence – as was the possession of a pack of playing cards (but I used to get round that one by laying out a pack of tarot cards). In the long run, his exploration of his gambling mania led on to a book, *The Psychology of Gambling*. His reading of Pascal and Dostoevsky, as well as Freud's analysis of Dostoevsky's novel *The Gambler*, led him to view gambling and religion as very similar, 'ways of controlling the ultimate authority of fate'. He regarded my Islam as a benign form of madness. Though he was an atheist, he had a terror of going to Hell and this must have been something that was dinned into him by his strict Baptist father. In arguing with me, he habitually turned passion into a rhetorical device. He used vehemence to intimidate anyone who seriously disagreed with him. At this stage he had yet to make his name as an art critic and well-known expositor of the ideas of John Berger.

It would be wearisome to list all the esoteric things I dipped into. Besides cults, I took up martial arts. Korean karate offered camaraderie and fierce discipline. Though one bowed ceremoniously at the opening of a bout, it was advisable to keep one's eyes on the opponent while doing so. The display of a single clawed finger meant that one wished to play it rough in this particular match. I was told by my teacher never to say that I was sorry, even if I had half killed my sparring partner. Also that you are not really into Korean karate until you have dreamed of killing someone with a Korean kick or blow. Later, I followed Korean karate up with aikido, a Japanese martial art which used locks and pressure against the joints. According to my teacher, 'In such combats there is neither victory nor defeat, for your opponent is your shadow and how can you defeat your shadow?' Though I was supposed to master the *Ki* force, I never even succeeded in identifying it. However, I did become adept at knee-walking.

Now the *Zawiya* seemed remote and unreachable. A *faqira* once told me that she could not decide whether the *Zawiya* was good or evil, for the hold that the place had over us felt cold and alien to her. Yes, it seemed to me then that no man can know for certain whether he is worshipping God or the Devil.

21. The tenth-century Sufi Shaikh al-Junayd

6

SHADOWS

I WAS IN MY SECOND YEAR at SOAS. Now that my grasp of the Arabic language was a little stronger, I was actually disappointed to discover how similar it was to European languages. In learning Arabic I had wished to acquire a second brain, or at least a new way of structuring how I saw the world and thought about it. At parties I used to lie about what I was studying, as it sounded so weird and because it would be tedious and difficult to explain why I was doing so. I could not imagine how to make medieval Arabic chronicles seem sexy. Therefore two of my fictional incarnations were as an officer with the Trucial Oman Scouts and as a professional mah-jong player. I was astonished to find how plausible I was.

My research drifted. In the mornings I used to sit up in bed, laboriously translating passages from late medieval Arabic chronicles while listening to *The Archers*. If, as sometimes happened, I was still in bed in the afternoon, then maybe I could listen to John Peel's *Perfumed Garden*. Even so, I generally rose from the bed and left the medieval texts scattered over the bedspread a little before lunchtime and strolled up to SOAS for a few games of pinball on the machine in the Junior Common Room. This was a pre-electronic, wooden contraption made by Gottlieb and its bumpers, rollovers and gates emitted satisfying clunking and thocking sounds. The iconography of the playfield and the backglass was based on some card game apparently being played on a paddle steamer on some river like the Mississippi. For some reason, pinball particularly appealed to SOAS's Sinologists and, as I played, I learned a lot about Chinese hermits, geomancy and the history of pyrotechnics. Once I had chalked up twenty replays, the maximum the machine could register, then I would walk away, leaving the replays for those who came after me, and I would go and have lunch. When the Who released 'Pinball Wizard' in 1969 my heart sang to the music.

Lunch was in the SOAS canteen. In those days it was not so wonderful and I fantasised that there must have been some educated Afghan warriors, hunched over their antiquated guns and looking down on the Khyber Pass, who reminisced about how terrible SOAS curries had been.

My Arabic improved more slowly than my pinball, but eventually I was able to read chronicles written in the Mamluk period (late thirteenth century to early sixteenth century) with a fair degree of ease. Some of these chronicles had never been printed, but survived as manuscripts written centuries ago that had ended up in the libraries of the British Museum, the Bodleian or the Bibliothèque Nationale. To read them was an eerie experience, since I knew that I was not their intended reader. Centuries ago, court scribes in Egypt and religious scholars in Syria had produced their annals in the expectation that their work would be read by fellow Muslims within a few years, or at most decades, after they had finished writing. Clearly their target audience was not a young British researcher who had been trained to read what they had written at cross-purposes to what they had intended. The court historians had produced panegyrics of their royal patrons and the religious scholars had dutifully logged the biographical details of fellow religious scholars whom they had judged to be reliable transmitters of tradi-tions concerning the Prophet and his Companions, but I went through all this material looking for evidence which might answer a modern historian's questions (about the economy, the organisation of the army, the conventions of chronicle writing and so forth) that it had not occurred to these medieval chroniclers to address.

As my Arabic improved, I stumbled across more interest-ing manuscripts, albeit ones which were perfectly irrelevant to my thesis topic. Abu'l-Qasim al-Iraqi was a thirteenth-century conjuror who also had pretensions to be a magician. Among his repertoire of spells was one for giving everybody in a room dogs' heads and another for fashioning sandals that could take one miles in just a few steps. He was also an alchemist and he made copies of the images and hier-oglyphics that he found in ancient Egyptian temples and then wrote alchemical commentaries on them. Ahmad ibn Zunbul al-Mahalli was a sixteenth-century Egyptian geo-mancer who could divine the future from marks in the sand. But he also wrote a (largely fictional) account of the down-fall of the Mamluks at the hands of the Ottoman Turks in the years 1516–17, as well as an illustrated cosmology which was full of marvels and accounts of secret treasure hoards. The Arab alchemist Ibn Umayl was another who sought to impose an alchemical reading on the ancient hier-oglyphs and my reading of what he actually wrote made obvious that Carl Jung had outrageously misrepresented him. It became clear to me without any shadow of a doubt that Jung was an intellectual charlatan, though, come to that, Ibn Umayl was also a charlatan. But Jung was also a racist and in his autobiography, *Memories, Dreams, Reflec-tions*, he had presented the Arabs as naïve, childlike and the ethnic dark shadow of the rational European.

With a handful of other advanced students, I attended a weekly class on the translation of medieval Arabic texts.

This was taught by John Wansbrough. He was one of the most remarkable men I have ever met. By then he had a white moustache and I thought that he looked like a plantation owner from one of the southern states of the USA and he did have the courtly manners that one associated with that sort of person. He was born in Illinois in 1928. He had studied at Harvard. He had been an outstanding rock climber and tennis player. A friend of Faulkner and Wittgenstein, he had served in the US Marines and worked for a while as a mining engineer. He became a lecturer at SOAS in 1960.

He was a formidable linguist and a great teacher. He was hard on students who were stupid or did not work, but he responded generously to signs of effort. One of the things that made him great was that he never troubled to conceal his perplexity when faced with a passage that was difficult to interpret. As a student in his class, I had the sense that I was standing right beside him at the pit-face of knowledge. 'Who knows what allusions lurk behind this apparently innocuous prose' was a typical remark of his. 'Clearly we have not decided what it means and that would be a pity if we had, for then it would cease to be interesting' was another. In cases of doubt, he absolutely refused to speculate. The sessions were also enlivened by his often cryptic and sarcastic remarks about his colleagues and rivals. Since I was doing a thesis on Mamluk history, I was shocked to hear him declare, somewhat contemptuously, 'No one has had a greater love affair with the Mamluks than David Ayalon.' According to Wansbrough, in Professor Hamilton Gibb's article on the subject in the *Encyclopaedia of Islam*, he 'assembled all the clichés on Arabic historiography'. Wansbrough was particularly scornful of the widely held view, promoted by Professor Montgomery Watt and others, that there were two phases in Muhammad's life. In the first phase, in Mecca, Muhammad was supposed to have been primarily a mystic and in the second phase, in Medina, Muhammad turned his hand to becoming a legislator. Wansbrough found the postulated chronology amusingly naïve.

He deployed a massive, polyglot vocabulary, both when writing and when speaking. I still have some of the notes I took during his classes and down their margins I had written words and phrases that were unfamiliar to me: metathesis, *Wissenschaft*, eponym, *locus classicus*, conflation, theophany, *Urquellen*, *Formenkritik*, backformation, aetiological, *evangelium infantiae*, *oratio recta*, asyndetic, parallelism, middle radical derivation, calque, *Heilsgeschichte*, paranoumasia and *hapax legomenon*. (Yes, I was still young and ignorant.) *Hapax legomenon* remains a great favourite with me.

He was not fond of students, nor of most of the staff. On one occasion I needed to get a job reference from him. So I found out the time and day of the class he was taking that term and waited outside the door at the time the class was due to end. The students all came out and I waited … and waited. Finally, I went into the classroom and found it empty. I went downstairs and conferred with the porter. 'Oh, that Wansbrough. He doesn't like being bothered by students. So he goes down the fire escape to avoid them.' The following week I waited at the foot of the fire escape. Though clearly surprised and bothered at being so trapped, he courteously agreed to write the reference on my behalf.

In the sixties he was an uncontroversial figure, for his thesis had been on Mamluk–Venetian commercial relations and he had yet to publish what seemed to be devastatingly deconstructive books about the origins of Islam. In *Quranic Studies* (1977) and *The Sectarian Milieu* (1978), he argued that the text of the Qur'an only achieved the form it did some two hundred years after the death of the Prophet and was the product of a prolonged intra-confessional debate.

So the Qur'an was a literary product, rather than a direct revelation of the divine. The ideas and the methodology were exciting and I am certain that Wansbrough put forward his interpretation of Islamic history in absolute good faith, but subsequent researches have demonstrated that his thesis is, almost certainly, wrong.

Though some thoroughly deconstructive ideas about the origins of Islam and the compilation of the Qur'an were put forward by Wansbrough and a few other scholars in the seventies, the best and latest evidence is that the Qur'an was written down quite soon after the Prophet's death and written down, moreover, in a form very close to the one we now have. Fragments of a Qur'an dating from the seventh and eighth century found in the Great Mosque in Sana'a in Yemen in 1972 differ in small details from the Qur'an as we have it today, but they nevertheless demonstrate that the idea that the text of the Qur'an evolved over a century or more, as a result of intra-confessional debate, cannot possibly be true. Moreover, it is possible that the textual differences between the Sana'a Qur'an and the one we have today may simply reflect the fact that the former is a bad copy. Still, it should be noted that, despite his extreme methodological iconoclasm, Wansbrough, like Zaehner a Catholic, believed that the Muslim revelation was in some sense true. Wansbrough's challenging theories about the origins of Islam never made me doubt the essential truth of my religion. 'The truth shall set you free' has been my watchword and I was confident that the essence of Islam would survive this peculiarly intense form of source criticism.

Wansbrough, who began his scholarly career by researching relations between Mamluk Egypt and Italy, told us that an academic should change his area of expertise every seven years. He was as good as his word, and, having changed from fifteenth-century diplomatic and commercial relations to Qur'anic studies, he subsequently moved on again and produced highly controversial interpretations of Ugaritic history. He also had ambitions to publish a novel. He did publish a short story in *Encounter*. As I remember, it read like a *sura* of the Qur'an rewritten by Kafka. Eventually he retired to his château in Montaigu-de-Quercy in the Lot valley of France and died in 2002.

The anthropologist who lodged in the same house as I did in Roupell Street put in my hands a cyclostyled paper by his thesis supervisor, Ernest Gellner, entitled 'Sanctity, Puritanism, Secularisation and Nationalism in North Africa: A Case Study'. This paper (first published in *Archives de sociologie des religions* in 1963 and reprinted in 1981 in Gellner's collected essays, *Muslim Society*) presented a sociological analysis of the life and works of Shaikh al-'Alawi. Gellner, early on in his career, had gained notoriety as a philosopher through his attack on Oxford linguistic idealism in *Words and Things* (1959). In 1962 he became Professor of Philosophy, Logic and Method at the London School of Economics. Meanwhile, however, he had switched his interest to anthropology and in *Saints of the High Atlas* (1969) he had studied the way saints in remote highland rural areas of Morocco had a political function as the mediator in conflicts between Berber tribesmen. He became famous as an intellectual polemicist and attacked fraudulent claims by Marxists and Freudians and, towards the end of his life, also those of Edward Said. I once met him in Cambridge and was struck by his intensity and the power of his intellect.

His reading of the life and works of al-'Alawi, for which his only source was Lings's *A Moslem Saint of the Twentieth Century*, is interesting. Lings, whose chief interest was in mysticism of the Perennialist kind, was treated by Gellner as if he was the innocent and unbiased provider of sociological data about religion in urban Algeria during the heyday of French colonialism. For Gellner, al-'Alawi's status as saint and shaikh militated against what he saw as one of the most fundamental aspects of Islam, the equality of all believers. Gellner, a committed atheist, offered a somewhat acerbic and at times sarcastic account of what both al-'Alawi and Lings stood for.

He presented al-'Alawi as a conservative and an outsider in the wider Islamic community. Al-'Alawi oscillated between egalitarian orthodoxy and esoteric elitism. His pamphlet *A Mirror to Show up Errors* revealed him to be a canny politician struggling against puritanical, rigorist critics. Gellner had no doubt that al-'Alawi's version of Islam belonged to the past and the future belonged to his critics: 'The future – if not the very distant future – lay with these puritanical, more Protestant, so to speak, religious teachers; they laid the foundations of the modern North African national consciousness in their struggle against religious particularism of those such as the Shaikh.' (But, as I write, the 'Alawiya flourish, while it looks as though the Puritan fundamentalists have been defeated in Algeria.)

For Gellner, the 'Alawiya, despite their urban centre, represented a Folk Islam with a cult of saints and a role in mediating between the individual and God. He believed that its opposite, Puritan Islam, was much better adapted to the modern post-colonial, globalising world. The latter was more egalitarian and carried less baggage. But I would say from personal experience that everybody was equal under the Shaikh and in that respect the 'Alawiya was a thoroughly egalitarian community. Moreover, Gellner's positing of an opposition between orthodox Puritanism and mysticism in this context is questionable, for the 'Alawiya were both puritanical and orthodox. Gellner looked at what was going on in Algeria in the early twentieth century through the wrong end of the telescope and he was unable to imagine any version of Islam as being anything more than the expression of sociological and political trends. He could not imagine that spirituality might have an independent value.

Here let me take a break from intellectuals and their books (as I often did then). Late one night, after a chance meeting with Kittoo and his girlfriend in the Joyboy, the Rasta café in Westbourne Grove, I broke open an ampoule of Methedrine (also known as speed) into a glassful of orange juice and after I had drunk it, having nothing better to do, I decided to walk back to Waterloo. Very soon and in a rush a chemically inspired and exultant brilliance seized me. As W. E. Henley put it:

I am the master of my fate:
I am the captain of my soul.

As I set out spring-heeled from Notting Hill a thousand possibilities presented themselves to my mind and then possibilities that stemmed from those possibilities and then more. Those proliferating possibilities were like branches that ramified in an infinite forest, in which I could effortlessly swing from branch to branch. I was inside my brain, so that I could admire the complex way in which it was structured. I was my perfect companion, for in the palace of mirrors within my head there were a thousand of me. And the 'me' was brilliant for it was obvious to me how time, consciousness and spirituality all connected. All the abstractions of the world were set out before me, as on a map, and all possible mental states were accessible to me. Introspection was the mighty engine through which I could control the world. I walked the length of St James's Park in what felt like seven-league boots. I travelled high on overblown metaphors. I rested on a bench, talking to myself like an aged philosopher who has seen too much of life.

As I crossed Waterloo Bridge, on the last stage of my walk across London, I felt myself to be possessed by a horrid mental energy and I thought that I could use this energy to draw in the clouds around me. The skin on my face was pulled very taut and I could feel a demon raging within me. To live at this level of intensity ... it felt as if the darkness, the clouds and the water were shaping themselves to my mood, for I was master of the elements. From somewhere I had acquired a treasured quotation: 'If you burn on earth, there will be nothing left for them to burn in Hell.' People slept but I, walking on alone, footman of the Apocalypse, cared for the world as it should be cared for. There were ghostly motorbike riders coming the other way, their wide pupils peering expressionlessly through goggles, their skulls sheathed in steel. They rode fast down the white line, playing chicken until the final encounter with the Omnipotent. But then their kick-seeking souls have been sucked from their frames like marrow from a bone and, God's zombies, they ride the highways to proclaim the awful, undesirable, last encounter. In my head the fierce jangling rhythms of the Velvet Underground provided the marching music of Methedrine.

The comedown from that drug is slow. Back in my room, I felt myself turning grey and I had the illusion that I was covered in dust, which the dawn light could not wash away. The mottling on the wall looked positively leprous and the cigar ash, rising and falling, fostered the illusion that I was living under a volcano. I kept checking with my watch to see that time was indeed passing. I could move only very sloooowly. I sat cross-legged on my bed, writing in a notebook, for ink was my anaesthetic. I now felt the alien chemical in my body. Though I had been up all night, sleep was beyond the possible. Methedrine is highly addictive and I took it half a dozen times. Long-term users are likely to lose all their teeth, mostly because of their excessively dry mouths. What did I think I was doing? It was perhaps a manifestation of the fatal power of my boredom to try to push me towards self-destruction. My body was a temple which I had filled with all sorts of strange things.

Of course 1968 was also the year of revolting students. There were sit-ins at the LSE and elsewhere and there were riots and strikes in Paris. I did not care about Vietnam. I actually thought the American domino theory (if Vietnam should be lost, then Cambodia and Thailand would follow, then Malaysia ...) was probably correct, but what did I know? I was wrong of course – wrong not to care and wrong to believe in the domino theory. Despite secretly hoping that the Americans would win in Vietnam, I perversely took part in the Grosvenor Square demonstration outside the American Embassy on 17 March. I was with a band of anarchists and I remember that one of them had brought a bag of marbles to roll under the police horses' hooves in an attempt to bring the horses down.

In May Harvey came and stayed with me and slept on the floor. Since my room was so very small, this made getting to the door difficult. I continued to argue with him. The craze for the Japanese game of Go was then at its height and consequently Harvey had taken to visualising arguments as so many games of Go, in which he sought to encircle the metaphorical black counters of the person he was talking to with his white counters and thereby win the debate.

I first met John Roe after going with Harvey to a screening of *Barbarella*. John looked a bit like John Ruskin and he lived in extreme poverty a little way off Tottenham Court Road. When I met him he had just been accepted as a probationer by a Hermetic cabbalistic order. He was barefoot since he was temporarily without his sandals, as they had been taken away to be consecrated in the Hermetic temple. He had been given various exercises to do, including lying in bed and remembering in the greatest detail possible everything that had happened to him. He also had to keep a diary which was to be inspected by his masters. A little later he left the Tottenham Court Road area to live in the vicinity of the Hermetic temple. There he was instructed on how to wrestle with new initiates.

A few months later, I re-encountered him, by which time he had left the Hermetic temple after having decided that it was in the service of evil. While he was there and for weeks afterwards he had felt his mind to be in thrall to the head of the order, the Magus. One day when John was there, the Magus came rushing out of the temple, yelling, 'That fucking horse! I can't get rid of that horse!' And indeed John could hear the horse in the temple neighing and kicking. But at least John learned to travel about in his astral body and, during one of his out-of-the-body trips around the house, he had encountered the Magus who was doing the same. My diary tells me that I spent many hours with John Roe, but I have no real memories of him. All this stuff was interesting at the time, but really it was the undergrowth of thought.

A friend from SOAS entered the Scientology headquarters on Tottenham Court Road and did their personality test. Although he deliberately and mendaciously answered every question in a positive, upbeat, healthy way, at the end of it he was told that the scores on his profile showed that he badly needed Scientology's help and that he would have to enrol on one of their expensive courses. I went a few days later and answered the questionnaire more honestly. After a week I received my results from an assured young man who told me that my answers were 70 per cent unsatisfactory. Unsatisfactory to whom, I wanted to know. He told me that I was acutely nervous, but also serene. We had an argument, with him arguing that total consciousness will protect an individual from all forms of accident or harm and me lecturing him on Freud's ideas about the psychopathology of error. He kept gazing directly at me as Scientologists are taught to do. Eventually he gave up trying to make me feel inadequate and he introduced me to a young woman whose job was to be the 'nice cop', corresponding to his 'nasty cop' act. She told me that I was very artistic, highly aware and startlingly honest … and would I not like to try an introductory course in Scientology? I walked out of their headquarters laughing.

However, some time later I enrolled at HQ to be audited, giving a false name and address, but a genuine telephone number. The auditing process involved me sitting with a couple of tin cans in my hands (a primitive sort of lie detector) while the auditor asked me questions. Inevitably there were attempts to get me to pay for more courses and for books. One evening I had a phone call from my auditor. As a matter of urgency he wanted me to come round to his flat near Goodge Street. I arrived an hour later and found him packing. He was defecting from the movement and since Scientologists have a ruthless way with those they term 'suppressives', he was going on the run and planning to hide out in Amsterdam. Since he was going to have to leave most of his stuff behind, I was welcome to choose what I wanted. As he continued to pack he talked about 'the wall of fire' that Scientologists have to go through, about the Incredible String Band's involvement and about what happened to suppressives.

I dropped in on many strange groups. It was not any part of a serious quest, but rather my hobby, since I believed (and still believe) that I had already found the truth in Mostaganem. My investigations into the mystical and the occult in London were partly amateur anthropology and partly sheer entertainment. But I learned some things. From a Zen master in London I learned how to sit properly. (If I did not, I was whacked on the back with a big stick.) From Krishnamurti and Sangharatshita I learned, I hope, to think and to express myself more clearly, for they both had beautiful minds. Yes, I was very bored indeed. Why is the world we are put upon so small? Just possibly if I had had a television things might have been different, but television in the sixties, with the exception of *The Prisoner*, was pretty terrible.

Sufi groups began to proliferate in Britain. No longer were they the preserve of Arab sailors in Cardiff or Tyneside. Now such groups were recruiting British seekers, especially young ones. Idries Shah, Inayat Khan, Dr Ross, Reshad Feilds and Ian Dallas were among those heading these Sufi orders. Some of these groups, such as the Darqawi one headed by Ian Dallas, strictly observed the prescriptions and proscriptions of Islam. But some other Sufi groups had only the most tangential relationship to Islam and the 'Sufism' was only a kind of brand label applied perhaps to lateral thinking or perhaps to some woolly New Age ethos.

Though I sensed that the Velvet Underground gave voice to my dark side, Donovan was the secular guru of my sunny side. Donovan's double album *A Gift from a Flower to the Garden* was released in April 1968 and by now I was ready to respond to him once more. Here everything was gentle, pretty and nice. People wore silks and sat about daydreaming in the sun. The music and the lyrics expressed the open wonder of being young as no other record of the time did. The first album, which was electric, *Wear Your Love Like Heaven*, was supposed to be for people who would one day be parents, while the second, which was acoustic, *For Little Ones*, was for the coming generation. For me the most potent track was 'Wear Your Love Like Heaven', in which the singer asked God for a kiss and in so doing evoked the name of Allah. When I hear it now 'Oh Gosh' summons up memories of the fashions of the time. On the second album, Donovan was experimenting with his recently mastered banjo and determinedly cultivating a childlike vision. Some of the album evoked a medieval and magical England in which one regularly encountered gypsies and tinkers, while other tracks dealt with a Victorian world that was passing away. Starfish and seagulls featured prominently. It is customary to compare Donovan to Dylan invariably to the former's detriment, but this is a pointless exercise. One might as well compare either or both to Buxtehude. Donovan travelled quite a different route from Dylan and it was the music of Donovan which had schooled me for love. Dylan was useless for that.

> To Carthage then I came, where a cauldron of unholy loves sung all about mine ears.
>
> (St Augustine, *The Confessions*)

This was the year of my last visit to Mostaganem. The ruins of Carthage are just a short distance up the coast from Tunis. That summer I met a couple of Arabic students from Durham University in Tunisia. Hearing that they were going out to Tunisia, their old school's classics master had implored them to 'Visit Carthage … and then spit on what is left of it!' In the summer of 1968 I was sent with a band of SOAS students to Tunis to study Arabic at the Institut Bourguiba. Classes started early in the morning, but were over by lunchtime. The class I found myself in was a visual treat, for not only were some of the British students beautiful, but the Spanish contingent, sent by their foreign office, also included some ravishing young women.

In the afternoons we generally went off to the beach at Sidi Bou Said. We took what felt like a toy train on a single-track line northwards along the coast, passing through La Goulette and Carthage. The village of Sidi Bou Said, so many white-walled, blue-shuttered houses, covered most of the hill that towered over the beach. Bougainvillea flowed over the garden walls and the scent of jasmine was everywhere in the alleys. A few boutiques of the kind one found on the King's Road had opened on the steep road that led to the summit.

Under a regimen of sun and sea, England fell away from me like a dead skin. The hawk-nosed ice-cream seller used to stagger along the beach, bent double under his load. The whites of his eyes burned in the shadow cast by his huge straw hat and he somewhat resembled a desperate castaway on a desert island. We desultorily worked at our Arabic and sang Beach Boy songs beside the glittering sea. *Pet Sounds* had been released this year and it was definitely the summer of the Beach Boys. Cumulatively the lyrics created what, in other circumstances, might have seemed a fantasy land of youth, sun, surf and golden girls, and yet that summer in Tunisia, we really were young and surrounded by sun, surf and golden girls. Wealthy American and European hippies had bought villas overlooking the beach and furnished them with Moroccan rugs, silk curtains and narghiles. They used to invite us in for drinks and hashish. It might be the Beach Boys on the record player, or it might be Bach's cello concertos. Michel Foucault, soon to become famous as a philosopher, was living in Sidi Bou Said at this time, and maybe we passed him on way up to the villas, but at this stage I had not even heard of him and I had yet to read his strange Nietzschean pseudo-history, *Folie et déraison: histoire de la folie à l'âge classique.*

I did the prayers and recited the *dhikr* when I was alone. Since Tunisia's president, Habib Bourguiba, had banned Sufi groups, they had to meet in secret, but I heard from a friendly Tunisian that on a certain night a Sufi circle was going to assemble in a graveyard on the outskirts of Tunis to recite the *dhikr*. On the night in question I made my way out of town down narrow alleyways infested by emaciated cats. A spur of rock rose high above the gravestones. The scimitar moon gave the only light as I climbed up the rock. I waited above the cemetery for the Sufis to appear, only they never did. Shadowy birds dipped and swooped below me. I sat hunched for hours on that rock looking across to the Bay of Tunis and imagined that I was shaping my future, spinning out my destiny. I sensed that this was another of the rare nights of power in which I was able to do this. Consequently, I felt no regrets at not having eavesdropped on a conventicle of Sufis.

In Tunis we slept in one of the university's dormitories under a naked light bulb. The sheets were soaked with sweat and covered with flies. Occasionally I would delay setting out to the beach and take a siesta, even though this was often literally a nightmarish experience. I would always fall asleep very rapidly. Losing consciousness was like falling through a trapdoor. In the first of several nightmares, I dreamed that, to amuse or instruct others, I was imitating a wild beast loping across a great marble hall. Suddenly I awoke from this to find myself in the dormitory in Tunis and through half-veiled eyelids I saw an arm (my arm?) resting on the sheet. But when I tried to move it, I could not. I tried to breathe and could not. I tried to laugh and then panicked. Then suddenly mind and body clicked together and I truly awoke in the same Tunisian dormitory. Nightmares visited me regularly in Tunis and a real nightmare is no mere bad dream, for it has specific and horrific qualities. As a Victorian treatise, *The Philosophy of Sleep*, puts it, the victim

may have the idea of a monstrous hag squatted upon his breast – mute, motionless and malignant; an incarnation of the evil spirit – whose intolerable weight crushes the breath out of his body, and whose fixed deadly incessant stare petrifies him with horror and makes his very existence insufferable.

In every instance, there is a sense of oppression and helplessness; and the extent to which these are carried varies according to the violence of the paroxysm. The individual never feels himself a free agent; on the contrary he is spell-bound by some enchantment, and remains an unresisting victim for malice to work its will upon. He can neither breathe, nor walk …

During my North African nightmares, I invariably became aware of the presence of the Other, a being who was somehow simultaneously and paradoxically dispas-sionate and malevolent. Whenever I could regain my voice, I would recite from the Qur'an to drive this creature away.

I was missing Methedrine. Though I had only taken it half a dozen times, the stuff exercised a powerfully addic-tive pull. But, thank God, I was travelling in lands where it was difficult, perhaps impossible, to get hold of this stuff. No other drug I tried had been so dangerous.

It had been fun singing Beach Boy songs on the sands below Sidi Bou Said, but I was impatient to move on to Mostaganem, for once again I was homesick for the *Zawiya*, with its minaret, fountain and pigeons. I left Tunis on 29 September. On the frontier I slept outside the Tuni-sian customs post and then in the morning I had to walk from the Tunisian customs to the Algerian customs post, a distance of about seven kilometres. In that no man's land I passed the carcass of a wild boar rotting majestically in the sun. I made the usual rough journey across Algeria. I slept on the floor of the police station in Constantine, for I had learned that impoverished travellers were entitled to be put up in police stations. I also slept in a gutter a little way out of Orléansville. After four days I reached Mostaganem, tired and very hungry. I was also apprehensive about return-ing to the *Zawiya* for the first time in two years.

But when I stepped into the courtyard Abdullah Faid turned and crowed with delight. 'The 'Alawi *Zawiya* is a form of spiritual vertigo. People are driven along the spiritual path by their imperfections. Moses was a murderer and David an adulterer ...' And he was off on one of his long chains of impromptu *mudhakarat*s. Faid, childlike but, to all intents and purposes, invincible, told me that he never knew what he was going to say until he heard himself say it. Perhaps he was addressing my ambition to be a saint when he told me quite dogmatically that saints were pointless. There was no use to them at all. One had to go out into the world.

That night, as I walked among the colonnaded shadows round the fountain of the *saha*, incandescent with a fiery longing, gazing at the stars set in the blackness beyond the minaret, I might well have been in Paradise. Paradise or not, I soon fell victim to dysentery and became very weak. I only rose from my sleeping bag for the prayers. I recovered fairly quickly, but then was overtaken by ecstasy, something that burned and that mingled pleasure and pain. When I tried to explain to 'Abd al-Qadir why it was I seemed to be so weak, his face brightened. '*Ah, la presse! La presse qui serre!*' All the *fuqara* experienced it. It was only important not to force it.

By now Faid had developed a craze for vitamin pills. They had an intoxicating effect upon him. Whenever he returned to his room after a decent interval, he was always careful to say '*As-salam aleikoum*'. This was his greeting to the jinn with whom he shared his room.

Every now and again, Faid would leave the *Zawiya* and head up into the hills. It was rumoured that he went there to get drunk, but he would never drink wine. Instead, he somehow managed to get drunk on old milk and dates, which would ferment in the stomach. This brew was called *nabidh*. Back in London, I tried this, but it did not work for me.

The only cinema in Mostaganem was owned by a *faqir* and, whenever there was a religious film, he let the *fuqara* in free. Faid went to see a film about the second Caliph of Islam, Umar ibn al-Khattab, and was childishly excited about it. Some years previously the Shaikh had sent Faid to Paris, where all the *fuqara* treated him with great respect as someone who was 'hot' from Mostaganem. Faid said '*Bien*' and then he looked in the mirror and declared 'Ah, Monsieur Satan, you are looking particularly fine today with your wonderful red beard and turban.' With that he clipped off his beard and threw off his turban. Then he realised that, despite this, he was still pure. So he went round the corner and bought some Gauloises and drank some wine before returning to the *fuqara*. Although Faid was celibate, this was unusual for a *faqir*. 'A *faqir* must go out into the world – not remain locked up, hidden away,' as he himself told me. Marriage and a job in the real world were enjoined for most of the *fuqara*. It was in some ways a cruel community. An (unholy) madman wandered into the *saha* one evening. The young *fuqara* teased him and knocked him about a bit, while Faid stood looking on and roaring with laughter.

Young 'Abd al-Rahman, a sixteen-year-old cousin of the Shaikh, was just beginning to grow a beard and was very keen on what he understood be the hippy thing and consequently he was known as 'Abd al-Rahman 'Ippy. After sharing some *shema* with him one afternoon, I watched him crunch up a couple of razor blades and display the fragments on his tongue before swallowing them. He told me that he could eat light bulbs as well. 'Not every day, you understand? Just now and then, to amuse my friends.' Eating glass was one of the specialities of the Aissawa and I assume he had learned the trick from them. 'Abd al-Rahman really admired the French weddings he had seen photos of in glossy magazines with the bride so beautiful in white and the wedding guests smart and decorous. He swore he would never be the victim of an Arab-style wedding with all the women ululating *you-you*s and the display of the bloody

22. Composite portrait of the first three Shaikhs of the 'Alawi order: Shaikh Hadj al-Mehdi, Shaikh al-'Alawi and Shaikh Hadj Bentounes

sheet. He asked me if there was a lot of sexual liberty in England. I hesitated and then said that, yes, I thought that there was. It was only after more conversation that I realised that, by 'sexual liberty', he meant men and women walking about together and maybe dancing.

A week or so after arriving at the *Zawiya* I had a brief audience with the Shaikh. I kissed his hand and he asked me if I was well and told me that he would see me soon. At that time he was rather preoccupied with the police, who kept turning up at the *Zawiya*, saying that they needed to investigate the accusations made by *El Moudjahid*. On my first Sunday in Mostaganem the Aissawa had marched past the *Zawiya* firing guns and bearing huge blue banners emblazoned with golden seal of Solomon. It was a demonstration against *El Moudjahid* and its editorials which attacked Sufis in general and the 'Alawis in particular. It was a sustained campaign. The *tariqa* was accused of peddling mystical nonsense, of meaninglessly chanting 'Allah', and the wearing of rosaries round the neck. *El Moudjahid* also attacked the practice of *khalwa* (even though this had been discontinued quite some time ago). The newspaper claimed that the candidate for solitary meditation was presented with a piece of card with the name of Allah written on it and he chanted 'Allah' for days or weeks until he thought he had received a vision. Often the name of God appeared before him lit up and hovering in the air. It was suggested that the candidates in *khalwa* were the victims of a conjuring trick based on the name of God being written in phosphorescent paint on a card that was covered up until the time was right and then the veil was pulled away.

The regional inspector of *habou*s (religious endowments) was particularly hostile to the 'Alawis. One of the points of contention was that 'Alawis had criticised the *'ulama'* (the mainstream religious scholars). Al-'Alawi was quoted as saying, 'Every member of the *'ulama'* should be considered by you to be Satan.' Also, the Shaikh was believed by his followers to be the Mahdi. (This last was probably true, though I am sure that the Shaikh gave no encouragement to this belief and indeed I was told by Faid that the Shaikh was looking for the Mahdi everywhere, seeking him in every person who was brought to see him.)

The Shaikh was alleged by the newspaper to use slave labour on his farm. His wealth came under scrutiny. He was accused of owning a Mercedes, a yacht, several farms, several printing presses, some butcher's shops and other sources of income. It is true that he was rich. A few years later, a friend of mine approached the British immigration authorities and asked if there would be any problem in the Shaikh becoming a British resident. Once they had checked on his wealth, they assured my friend that there would be no problem at all in his coming to settle in Britain. Effectively he was royalty.

The *Zawiya* was obviously a nest of CIA spies. According to *El Moudjahid*, the *tariqa* was a sinister international organisation, for there were 'Alawi *zawiya*s in Algiers, Oran, Tizi Ouzou, Ghaza, Tunis, Rabat, Paris, London, Liverpool, Brussels, Lausanne and elsewhere.

In Mostaganem the Shaikh was perceived by the FLN and their thugs to be dangerous and very cunning. He was alleged to have several government officials in his pocket. He was known to receive mysterious visitors late at night. And why were so many foreigners coming to the *Zawiya*? That had to be suspicious. The Jeunesse 'Alawiya, headed by the eighteen-year-old Khaled, was denounced as being a separatist organisation and moreover one which was super-fluous, since there already was an FLN youth organisation. *El Moudjahid* ended up by accusing the 'Alawiya of being a state within a state and its campaign reached a crescendo with demands that the Shaikh be sent to prison. The man making this demand was an ex-*faqir* who had a grudge against the Shaikh and who had since risen to become Min-ister of Religion. But the *fuqara* spent weeks praying for the survival of the *Zawiya* and after some weeks they heard that the minister had been removed from his post and the hostile campaign came abruptly to an end. For a time that is, but things were to take a more sinister turn in the following year.

That summer there were many tensions in the *Zawiya*. There were people in the town who thought that I was a spy. But Faid and Selima were even more suspect since they were also Europeans and they spent so much more time than me at the *Zawiya*. This was the year I encountered Selima, a middle-aged Frenchwoman who had clearly been very attractive in her youth. She kept a copy of *Les Oeuvres spir-ituelles de St Jean de la Croix* at her bedside. Our conversa-tion was mostly quite banal and unspiritual. She claimed to have the ability to read auras. (However, my friend Ben Wint, who had spent time in a Buddhist monastery in Thai-land and who was up in auras, once observed that one could not read all that much in auras – no more than a normally sensitive person could deduce from looking at a face.) Selima's French name was Pierette Guy. 'Pierette' had been the last word her mother had uttered before expiring in labour. Selima had had a tough life as an orphan and then married a feckless artist who deserted her. But now she ran a profitable hairdressing salon in Saint-Germain. Yet she was still able to visit the *Zawiya* for eight or nine months at a time.

Selima loved Ramadan, the month of fasting, and during the previous Ramadan she had had a wonderful vision of the Virgin May ascending to Jesus from the Mount of the Assumption. She had been visiting the *Zawiya* for seven years. On the day of her conversion to Islam she had donated 10 million old francs to the *Zawiya*. She acted as a guru to young females who arrived at the *Zawiya*. I gathered that the women under her tutelage tended to pray irregularly at odd hours and on their own. According to her, appearances of the dead were mere psychic detritus doomed to disappear quite quickly. A propos of I cannot remember what, she told me the story of a friend of hers who went to a party in Paris. At the party were also a newly married Belgian couple. One after another, all the male guests slept with the bride. Next morning the couple committed suicide. She and Faid were constantly at odds. She believed that Ahmed (that is Harvey) had acquired many devils from a previous incarnation (but I should point out that reincarnation is no part of the Islamic faith). In retrospect, I can see that she did not like Harvey, or me. Harvey, by the way, was elsewhere in the Middle East and he was never to return to the *Zawiya*. Faid had told me that one should seek out people who were difficult to get on with, for they would be the people whom it would be good for me to know. On that basis, I should have got to know Selima a lot better.

As had been the case with the early Franciscan Order, the *Zawiya* was riven by personal rivalries and factions. Selima

23. A group of *fuqara*, probably Moroccans, on a visit to the *Zawiya* in Mostaganem

was reputed by the men to be forever plotting to influence the Shaikh. She was reported to be anti all men, but, apart from her rivalry with Faid, she had a particular feud with 'Abd al-Qadir, why I do not know. 'Abd al-Qadir was an enormous man, quite intimidating to look at – swarthy, muscular and black-bearded, resembling a Barbary corsair. He had been '*le plus grand bandit d'Alger*', a former boxing champion in that city, and had been involved in some racketeering, I think. But then he repented when the Shaikh found him weeping beside his father's grave in an Algiers cemetery and he was moved to tell the Shaikh the details of all his crimes. The Shaikh turned to his followers and said, 'You see how men are.' 'Abd al-Qadir now had a reputation as a very good man, though narrow in his views. He had moved to Oran. I think that he worked as a demolition man, though his technique, as he described it, seemed practically suicidal. He would walk into a building, set light to the fuse of a stick of dynamite and then throw it up in the air shouting, '*Allahu akbar! Boom!*', then he would repeat

191

the process until he was able to walk out from the ruins of the building. He told Harvey how he used to go fishing in a small boat in the early morning, but one morning when he started to fish he saw the fish saying their prayers, so he overturned his boat and swam back to the coast and never went fishing again. He had received no formal education, but he told me that he received all the instruction he needed from the Shaikh in dreams. He campaigned against the influence of Selima and other women in the *Zawiya*. 'Abd al-Qadir told me that what he esteemed about me was that I liked to do the *'imara* and he gave me lots of mystical advice. He also demonstrated how to lift a chair with one's teeth.

A little later the tensions in the *Zawiya*, not just the quarrel between 'Abd al-Qadir and Selima, but concerning other matters that I cannot write about, led to an exceptionally fierce *'imara*. This had been widely predicted by the *fuqara*. By the time the dance was in its fourth round I was moving like a corpse with no volition of my own and a reddish gold light exploded in my head, just before I felt the Otherness coming to get me and, as it entered my body, it seemed to me that it wished to destroy me utterly. For an instant I welcomed it, but only for an instant. Then I was crying silently, 'No, no, no, no, no …' At the same time I could hear my actual voice making the strangled cry of one who has gone *melboos*. Though I wanted to drop to the floor, my neighbours in the dance held me firmly upright. Only, just as the dance finished, minutes or seconds later, did 'Abd al-Qadir thrust me to the ground. As the *fuqara* continued to chant, I found myself staring at the carpet and thinking, 'Coward, coward, coward …' and my sweat flowed over the carpet. Afterwards 'Abd al-Qadir told me that I had performed the *'imara* well, too fast, but still well. 'You felt something, then?' he asked, an eye closing in a cynical corsair's wink, before he burst into a roar of delighted laughter. When, a day or two later, I asked him about the nature of *melboos*, he just said it was good thing, an aspect of holy madness, before repeating the trick of holding a chair by his teeth.

That summer one of the *fuqara* who lived nearby got married. On Friday there was Arab music and dancing. On the Saturday the bride was examined by women from the bridegroom's family and a little later the wild ululation further up the street confirmed that she was a virgin. In the evening, after a rather sparse feast of couscous with pieces of chicken and sprinkled sugar (for this *faqir* was literally poor), we assembled outside the *Zawiya* and, arm in arm and supplied with candles, flowers and fireworks, we advanced chanting up the street and paraded round the main square of Tijdit. Then we sang a chant of blessing in the bridegroom's house, before moving on to the roof of a neighbour's house, where we sang more 'Alawi songs, drank mint tea and ate cakes. 'Abd al-Rahman 'Ippy surreptitiously smoked a cigarette and I took *shema*. This was all quite colourful, but later the younger *fuqara* told me that they did not like this sort of thing. Like 'Abd al-Rahman 'Ippy, they preferred the European style of wedding.

That night an agonising toothache kept me up and pacing about on the roofs of the *Zawiya*. A wisdom tooth was trying to push its way up through my gum. At four thirty in the morning I went up to the square where there was a café open and an old man bought me café au lait. I asked him about dentists. He wanted to drag me along to the local miracle worker, an electrician who had been cured of paralysis at Medina, and who had miraculous powers at pulling out teeth. I had to flee. The pain gnawed at my head so much that it was hard to think. A little later in the day Faid tried to propel me to the approved dervish dentist. He would have walked me into the sea and, after reciting a passage from the Qur'an, he would have used a pair of pincers to yank out whichever he guessed to be the offend-ing tooth. I went to the hospital in Mostaganem proper, but there was a queue and the dentist was not expected for a day or two. I then resorted to the most powerful pain-killer that a chemist was prepared to sell me and it, called Cibalgine I think, was indeed powerful. When finally I came off this stuff I was delirious. I crawled about on my hands and knees in one of the rooms off the *saha*, shouting out things like, 'Avast there, Mr Starbuck! Dost see the white whale?' The *fuqara* looked on mystified. Even when I did not have toothache, I was feverish a lot of the time during my sojourn at the *Zawiya* that summer.

On 20 August Soviet tanks rolled into Prague. I remem-ber a pair of aged *fuqara* sitting on the floor, leaning against a wall, reading about it in *El Moudjahid* and, for all I know, deducing apocalyptic consequences from it. On 23 August I sang 'Happy birthday to me' in the *saha* on a cold grey morning. It was a bleak birthday, as I was full of doubts about the right spiritual path. Within the *Zawiya* I could doubtless lead a life of perfect holiness and, indeed, it would be easy, but how would it be when I returned to England? I took to sleeping in front of the tomb of the Shaikhs, as I hoped to be guided by good dreams, but none came.

Towards the end of my stay in Mostaganem, I was sum-moned to the local Commissariat de Sécurité and subjected to a barrage of questions. Why was I here? Why had I con-verted to Islam here rather than in England? Who were my parents? What political, social or economic circles did I move in back in England? It went on and on. It was plain that I was suspected of being a spy for the CIA. (I do not think that they had heard of MI5.) Part of the problem was that there was a local prejudice against the notion that one could be a Muslim and yet not be a Moroccan or an Alge-rian national.

That same evening, after I had returned from my

interrogation, the Shaikh summoned me to his quarters. He waited for me on a deckchair on the balcony and his interrogation was worse than that of the FLN's security goons. First, he wanted to know about what the Commissariat had asked me. Somehow Selima had found out that I had been taking drugs in England and that I had fallen into bad company and she reported this to the Shaikh. He was coldly furious. I was under strict instructions to break with disreputable friends in England. I was to follow a routine which involved performing all the prayers with supplementary *rakat*s and reading the Qur'an all day, except for eating, praying and sleeping and an afternoon walk. I could not be entrusted with a *dhikr*. I submitted, for indeed I feared the Shaikh. It was a Thursday evening and the time of the regular reunion, but shaken, I did not perform the *'imara* that evening. For the first time, I watched it from the outside and it looked frightening. It looked like a ring of corpses animated by the terrible power of the name of God. Looking back on my time in Mostaganem that summer, I wrote in my diary that I had had a wretched time.

I resumed my intensive study of the Qur'an and I wrote chunks of it down in my notebook in English and in Arabic. I paused over the grim threats of the judgement to come. It seemed that I was under an exacting God and one whose messages to the world he had created were bafflingly cryptic. What was the Lote Tree at the furthest limit? What was the Holy Screaming? Was my heart uncircumcised? I was to consider everything in the world around as signs from God that pointed to something else. After one afternoon of such study I paced up and down on a roof beside the *saha*. The air shimmered so brilliantly that it felt as if it was some kind of warning aura and that some kind of fit was imminent. The sky, sea and bulrushes showed so clear and bright as if they were the background to a story from the Bible re-enacted in a vision. The minaret, like a finger of admonition, loomed over me. It was Sunday, a little before the noon prayer, and few people moved in the street, but those that did seemed like isolated figures in a mysterious parable – the holy fool, the beggar, the sinful woman, the lamed man and the muezzin.

A little later I staggered to the top of a hill outside town and collapsed, as a fountain of fire seemed to be forcing my breast apart and the sky and sea threatened to fold in on me. I bit my arm as I contemplated the Essence and sought helplessly to grasp something beyond the manifestation of the visible. Finally I cooled down sufficiently to look down on the dying blades of grass and the snail shells that lay littered all around me. Earlier that afternoon, the children of Tijdit, perhaps sensing that I was in a strange state, had twice stoned me – usually the treatment reserved for holy fools, full-blown madmen and unlucky animals.

Towards the end of my stay in Mostaganem, 'Abd al-Qadir and Selima had left, Faid had run out of *mudha-karat* and the Shaikh was not receiving me. How could one possibly be bored in such a place? But yet I had become bored. I felt as though I had lost everything. The toothache continued to rage on, barely muffled by the dangerously powerful painkillers. After only a few weeks in the *Zawiya*, eating a bun or reading a four-week-old newspaper felt like the height of sensual pleasure. I was homesick and I missed television, cigars, Donovan on the record player, the *Times Literary Supplement*, cornflakes, curries, salads, toasted cheese and normal human behaviour.

The Shaikh had been away for a week or so. It was rumoured that he had gone to Paris to receive treatment for his heart. When he returned, accompanied by a retinue of Parisian *fuqara*, I sought an audience with him. He received me in his favourite place, the garage. I kissed his hand and sought permission to return to England. He replied that he would see me in the afternoon. Only then was I given permission to go. As I sat under the stars in the *saha* that evening, I was exceptionally melancholy. Somehow I had failed to achieve what I should have and, though I did not know it, this was the last time that I would ever set foot in the *Zawiya*.

The hitchhike to Algiers was an easy one. That evening I sought out 'Abd al-Qadir in the Hussein Dey quarter. He and his family lived in a cramped flat in a massive apartment block. We sat up late at night talking. He deplored the factions that were tearing the *Zawiya* apart and depriving the Shaikh of proper support. That night for the first time in many weeks I actually slept in a bed. From Algiers I hitched on back to Tunis. On the way I stocked up with tins of *shema*. The hitchhiking continued to be easy and at one point a Tunisian policeman insisted on doing the thumbing for me. From Tunis I flew back to London.

Several weeks after my return to London, I wrote an apologetic letter to the Shaikh. I learned through various intermediaries that he had been forced to dissolve the Jeunesse 'Alawiya. The FLN's menaces were becoming more frequent.

In December 1968 Lindsay Anderson's film *If...* was released. I went to see it in London the week it was released. The audience was packed out with ex-public school boys and when the film finished most of us rose to give it a standing ovation. We cheered the massacre with a Gatling gun of the assembled teachers, parents and boys. Like so many other films of the sixties, *If...* celebrated a youthful adversarial stance in relation to the rest of the world.

There were eerie similarities to my own school: the big trunk that had to be unpacked at the beginning of term; the eccentric English master; the files left on the steps of the chapel; the homosexual pashes; the wearisome Officer Training Corps exercises with Lee Enfield rifles;

the oppressive prefects in control of the houses; the toast prepared on a two-bar electric fire; the waistcoats that only prefects could wear; the shouts that summoned small boys to run to do some fagging; the savage beatings. In my house, the house beatings took place in the bathroom next to the dormitory after lights out. So the victim would be summoned from his bed and make his way in the dark towards the door where the prefect was waiting with the cane in his hand. The rest of us would lie shivering in our beds, counting the strokes. There was a hierarchy of beatings: a prefect's beating, the head of house's beating and the house master's beating (these two were of roughly equal status), the head prefect's beating and, finally, the headmaster's beating. This last was flamboyantly performed with a whippy cane on the stage of Big School in front of all the boys. It was not done to blub and, indeed, once the beating was over, one was expected to thank the prefect or master from whom one had received the caning. The film held up a mirror to my schooldays.

But the bullying that I remember so well from my school did not feature in *If* …. The boys at my school created a hell for themselves. It was boring to sit reading *Lord of the Flies* in class, for that sort of tribalism, violence and singling out of scapegoats was already familiar to us as part of our daily existence at school. When, a few years after the release of *If*, I was imprisoned as a suspected pro-Palestinian terrorist in Jerusalem, it did not seem so bad. I was used to confinement. I was used to sharing a room with twenty other people. I was inured to lack of privacy on the toilet, bad food and a strict regimen. So far so good, but still that school had destroyed my childhood.

My youth was scudding away in a benighted quest for heightened awareness. In a diary from this year I wrote: 'As long as the Truth can be denied, it must be denied.' I was busy then coining aphorisms, most of which are far too boring and senseless to be set out in print. But it was around this time that I had the idea that the real purpose of keeping a diary might be to make a literary selection of things that happened to me and, in so doing, turn my life into a work of art, a future novel.

24. Abraham preparing to sacrifice Isaac

7

AFTERMATH

UNLIKE HARRY HALLER, I never learned to foxtrot. But in any case, as the sixties progressed, the music became more difficult to dance to. It was impossible to dance to 'I'm Waiting for the Man' or 'White Rabbit'. Still, the driving rhythms of such music drove my pacing about backwards and forwards across London. Some records gave rhythm and sentiment to my romantic despair, but others, such as Jefferson Airplane's *Surrealistic Pillow*, or those of Hapshash and the Coloured Coat, worked better as spirit guides for trips on drugs.

At that May Ball in the summer of '67 the Who had performed 'I Can See for Miles', a song about sexual betrayal. Even so, for me the music which became the dirge that accompanied Juliet's departure and which even now still preserves some melancholy power is not anything by the Who, but Prokofiev's *Romeo and Juliet*. (Hand in hand in the cinema, Juliet and I had watched Paul Czinner's film version of the ballet with the Kenneth Macmillan choreography.) It took me a long time to get over Juliet and, after she had left me, the doom-laden heavy tread of 'The March of the Knights' from that ballet became my personal anthem of lost love.

There is a saying attributed to Abu Mihjan, a Companion

of the Prophet: 'If you drink wine, let it be the finest; if you listen to music, let it be the sweetest; and if you commit a forbidden act, let it be with a beautiful partner, so that, even though you may be convicted of sin in the next world, you will not at any rate be branded as a fool in this.' After Juliet, I went out with a series of strikingly good-looking women and, though I never got very far with any of them, in retrospect I think that I was blessed to be able to drink in their beauty. Only it did not feel quite like that at the time, for I was in torment, but yet I delighted in that torment.

The first girlfriend after Juliet was a fey, slender blonde with a marvellously husky voice and I was not the only one who thought that she looked like Mia Farrow. I took her to Middle Earth to dance to Pink Floyd and the Crazy World of Arthur Brown. This was followed by a gentle flirtation with an English rose. Then there was a tall, dark-haired, precariously sane young woman with high Slavic cheekbones and a long black leather coat of the sort an SS officer might have worn. After that, I had a tormented affair with a very sexy Kenyan Asian law student, here to be called Ayesha. She thought I was good-looking but quite stupid and, like Juliet, she used to tease me relentlessly. On balance, I was more flattered than annoyed by being rated as a good-looking dimwit, even though it was more common for my girlfriends to credit me with neurotic brilliance. I was usually thought to be sweet and gentle, but the women I went out with, in the end, almost always preferred their men to be hard and arrogant.

There were other less serious encounters with women. I was rereading Proust at this time and found that he had produced an encyclopedia of betrayals and emotional break-ups, as his sequence of novels detailed obsession, paranoia, jealousy, ambivalence, fantastic fears and hopes and the final incommensurability of different emotional states. Indeed, I wondered if my earlier reading of Proust at

Oxford had not somehow been responsible for sabotaging all my subsequent ventures into the realm of love. Proust's great book might have hard-wired me for emotional failure.

According to a saying of the Prophet: 'The game of a man with a woman is one of the games that the angels like to watch.' According to the thirteenth-century Andalusian mystic Ibn al-'Arabi: 'To see God in the form of a woman is the most perfect vision of all.' Again, according to Ibn al-'Arabi: 'Whoever knows the worth of women and the mystery reposing in them will not refrain from loving them; indeed love for them is part of the perfection of a man who knows God, for it is a legacy of the Prophet and a Divine Love.' I do not want forty virgins in Paradise. Virgins are hard work. Still, the sensuality of the Muslim Paradise seems to me to be one of the best features of Islam. I think that, when I was young, I was more afraid of women than I was of God. Even so, it was and is easy to love them. But how do people find it possible to love something so vast, so terrifying and so incomprehensible as God? Why does God need our love and our worship anyway? It is one of the many things I do not understand. The love of an ant for a human being would not be more bizarre than the love of a human for God.

But perhaps a man's or a woman's love of God is a form of Mad Love. The Surrealists were keen on Mad Love and André Breton published *L'Amour fou*, a novel which can be read at another level as a mystical treatise. In this autobiographical fiction the mysteries and revelations of love are concealed in the mundane. As it happens, the modern Syrian Arab poet Adonis divined that there are overlaps at many levels between Sufism and Surrealism. The Sufi and the Surrealist are engaged on a quest within an interior world. As the poet put it in his strange and difficult book *Al-Sufiyya wa'l-Surriyaliyya*:

Like the Sufis, the Surrealists use intuition and the way of life as a source of illumination, in their pursuit of knowledge, as opposed to rational and logical methods and in contravention of them. They regard reason as a shackle that only controls them by enchaining them.

We can also see that for both the Sufis and the Surrealists, the dream does not lie completely outside reality, nor is it estranged from it. Dream and reality are, in fact, two sides of the same truth; they incorporate the visible and the invisible.

We can also see that both Sufis and Surrealists regard writing as an experience that connects the visible to the invisible.

Both movements have been sources of great creativity. Both paths involve suffering. 'Love is a torture. Love kills.'

Since I was intensely and articulately neurotic, this must have been off-putting for the succession of girlfriends. I hoped that I could impress them with my intensity, for it was all I had. I wept alone, for I suffered fits of intense depression and eventually I was referred to a psychoanalyst who had a clinic in Mayfair. He hated mysticism and hated the way I dressed in black. He told me that my main problem was that I wanted to excel at everything and that I was obsessed with not being ordinary. He implied that my emotional and sexual immaturity was a sort of penalty that I had to pay for my spiritual and intellectual pride. I was not prepared to accept the dullness of other people's everyday reality, but this was what I was going to have to do.

The psychoanalysis had to be discontinued in the summer of 1969, when I joined a university geological expedition to what was then the Trucial States (shortly to become the United Arab Emirates). The geologists were going to investigate the phenomenon of the singing sand dunes and I was to be their interpreter. We drove through Europe and

Anatolia in a battered old army lorry to cross into Iran. When we reached Tehran, Tony Hutt, who was temporarily in charge of the British Institute of Persian Studies, put us up in the institute's compound and garaged the lorry. It was Tony who introduced me to two musicians who were members of the Sufi Ne'mutullahi Safialishahi order and, after spending an evening with them, I was given an initiatic handshake, for they had recognised that I was a fellow Sufi. South of Shiraz the geologists I was with mistook a dried-up riverbed for a road and consequently we had a rough journey down to the port of Bandar Abbas. There we encountered an American Peace Corps worker who was six foot eight inches tall. His height had saved him from being sent to Vietnam, as it would have been too much trouble to make a uniform to fit him. He invited us to dinner in the small castle on the very edge of the sea. After dinner he put *Scheherazade* on the record player, so that the music of Rimsky-Korsakov, a programmatic symphonic suite about adventure, romance and the sea, mingled with the lapping of the waves against the castle's stones. At the port we had the lorry loaded on to the deck of a dhow, where it was surrounded by goats, and we sailed on to Dubai, a pleasing little town of white-walled houses with the traditional wind towers. The expedition was a failure at two levels. The singing sand dunes would not sing for us and my Arabic was not up to Gulf colloquial, in which k becomes ch, q becomes g and j sometimes becomes y. I just could not perform the substitutions quickly enough in my head and, besides, I was not used to actually speaking Arabic. But it was an interlude of moonlit harbours and overlit deserts. I liked the heat and it was pleasant to reread Proust in the Empty Quarter.

I did not feel that psychoanalysis was delivering answers that I wanted to hear and so the sessions with the doctor in Mayfair were never picked up on again. In seeking help from psychoanalysis, I had been following Peter Fuller's example. For some years more he continued to monitor and comment on my emotional life with perhaps a touch of Schadenfreude. In the seventies he was living with his first wife, Colette, and his pet axolotl in a scruffy flat in Dalston. While espousing the ideas of the left-wing art critic and novelist John Berger, Peter wrote for the short-lived Marxist glossy weekly *Seven Days*. But subsequently he discovered Ruskin's exposition of what was really a Victorian interpretation of medieval values. As Julian Stallabrass has suggested, 'Ruskin was a restless, comprehensive intellectual and fine prose stylist, he was moralistic, a purveyor of elevated journalism, ill at ease with his epoch and his sexuality and somewhat mad; all these qualities suited him in the role of Fuller's alter ego.' Peter's adoption of Ruskinian ethics and views on craftsmanship eased his movement towards the right and what one of Peter's friends, the art critic Andrew Brighton, has termed 'Establishment philistinism'. I was disappointed, though not surprised, by the rightward drift. Those dinners with Maurice Cowling and other high Tories and Anglo-Catholics had at last borne fruit.

Eventually, Peter and I fell out. As he began to move in intellectual celebrity circles, we saw less of each other. When *Images of God: The Consolations of Lost Illusions* was published in 1985, he had a big launch party to which I was not invited. Then I, in my role as the bad fairy Carabosse, reviewed the book in *Time Out* and, after noting the diversity of its contents, remarked on the reactionary drift: 'What gives the unity is that whether Fuller is banging on about Rothko or aborigine art, sooner or later Ruskin and his blessed cathedrals crop up.' I noted how he had passed from one enthusiasm to another – Freud, Marx, Berger, Ryecroft, Winnicott and now Ruskin. 'Where next? I am putting my money on St Ignatius of Loyola.' The review concluded: 'Who is our best and most interesting art critic today? Peter Fuller unfortunately.' We never spoke again and, though I often had dreams in which we re-encountered one another and patched things up, this never happened. He married into money and, in a way, this proved to be his doom, for in 1990, while he was being driven down to London for an interview of some kind, his chauffeur fell asleep on the motorway and Peter was killed in the ensuing crash.

As Danny observes in one of the final scenes of the film *Withnail and I*, 'They're selling hippy wigs in Woolworth's, man. The greatest decade in the history of mankind is over. And, as presuming Ed here has so consistently pointed out, we have failed to paint it black.' *Easy Rider* was released in 1969. Towards its end the character played by Peter Fonda declares, 'We blew it.' Clearly the hippy sixties ended in anticlimax, but one needs some perspective here. Only a few young people had ever bought into the hippy ethic, which was in any case poorly articulated. Moreover, to take music as an example, over the decade Cliff Richard, Engelbert Humperdinck and *The Sound of Music* were all more successful than the Beatles. The sixties turned out to be all trousers and no mouth, for the fashions were fine, but there was very little in the way of worthwhile literary production and no one produced a persuasive manifesto of what the hippies might stand for. Then there were so many gods that failed. There were the spiritual gurus, like the Maharishi and other charlatans that I have either already named or am shortly about to discuss. But there were also secular charlatans, like R. D. Laing, Herbert Marcuse, Marshall McLuhan, Timothy Leary and Ivan Illich. And drug-taking went nowhere. In the end, it and the culture it supported came to seem boring. A friend, who, like me, had tried most of the iconic drugs of the decade, confided that he had come to the conclusion that the best drug with the most predictable highs was alcohol. It was a bonus that it was amazingly easy to score alcohol and there was no fear of being busted by the fuzz.

It was, in Donovan's words, 'The Season of the Witch'. On the whole, the British working man shunned the occult and the esoteric. Wealthy and titled people, who were otherwise idle, dabbled in these things, as if they could thereby further confirm their elite status. I met quite a few well-heeled esotericists and did not particularly care for them (though of course I was also idly dabbling). The gurus commonly brandished dodgy doctorates and bogus lectureships and they were rumoured to have performed miracles, though under what circumstances was hard to track down. Quite a few of these holy men turned out to be sexual predators. Much of the charlatanry was modelled on that of earlier charlatans such as Blavatsky, Besant, Crowley and Gurdjieff. There was a lot of talk about the coming of the Age of Aquarius, but, as the sixties gave way to the seventies, challenging and experimental aspects of some of the cults shaded down into the pastel colours and woolly thinking of the New Age. Hard-hat, fast-thinking and analytical, I spied on people who were not.

In 1970, not long before he left for the Middle East, Harvey moved into Centre House and I used to frequently visit the place while he was there. Centre House was a utopian commune in Notting Hill presided over by Christopher Hills, who was, like Schuon, a charismatic character with a beard. Everyone took it in turns to cook the meals and eating them was a solemn exercise, for the first mouthful one took had to be meditated on with eyes closed for five minutes. (I guess that, if one persisted long enough with the same morsel of food in one's mouth, one would achieve some sort of gastronomic jamais vu.) Hills believed that the world's nutritional problems could be solved by getting the poor of the Third World to eat algae. Under his direction, trees and lemons were tested with an e-meter, though I can no longer remember for what. In the evenings there were meditations, exercises in silent communication and blind feeling – so many techniques for raising consciousness. (But what would one do with a raised consciousness when one had it? Do we really need raised consciousnesses?) Hills and his chief disciples tried to teach us to sense auras and to detect the mass and colour of objects by blindfold sensing. Hills lectured on instances of telepathy in the New Testament and from him I learned that the colour blue is not mentioned once in the Bible. The group was very much into things like the Luscher colour test, which assessed your personality on the basis of your favourite colour. The trouble was that in those days I was under the impression that my favourite colour was red, whereas in reality it is yellow. Then there was an inevitably ghastly truth game, where, one after another, we entered the circle and then those around delivered uncomfortable truths. The people at Centre House perceived me as being very aloof and intellectual, and so I was, I suppose.

The increasing ease of air travel not only made it easier to visit gurus in India, but it also made it easier for them to come to Britain. Once he had moved to the Middle East and thereby escaped from a sea of troubles in Britain, Harvey wrote to me about how worried he was that so many of our friends were vanishing into a cult called the Divine Light: 'innumerable countless multitudes of my one-time friends and acquaintances falling victim to its deadly charm [*sic*]'. The Divine Light's founder, Guru Maharaj Ji, came over to Britain in the seventies and instructed his followers to meditate on the holy name. I also heard from one of them that they had to monitor the whistling sounds in the head. It was a cult that made great social and financial demands on its followers and it seemed a bit sinister the way people vanished into the Divine Light. Later there were instances of anti-cult activists kidnapping disciples and deprogramming them to free them from the brainwashing they had allegedly been subjected to.

Transcendental Meditation, which arrived in Britain around 1967, seemed more benign. It had been publicised by the Beatles, who went to India soon after the release of *Sgt. Pepper* and sat at the feet of the giggling Maharishi Mahesh Yogi. Donovan also came with them. The Maharishi had three mantras to offer his followers and, if one repeated these enough, enlightenment would follow. In the shorter term, a small degree of levitation might be possible. I heard a rumour that people who did Transcendental Meditation were having their energy drained by the Maharishi's deceased master, who was using it for battles in the astral world. To me this sounded like a plot detail from one of the *Doctor Strange* comics that I used to read in those days. The public teaching about universal harmony sounded soppy and vague. Still, I enjoyed the company of SOAS students who were into Transcendental Meditation (and Buda, if you are reading this, do get in touch).

I met J. G. Bennett several times at Sherborne House in the Cotswolds. He dressed in tweeds. By then in his seventies, he was balding and a little vague and he seemed to doze off when anyone except himself was holding forth. But his eyes were those of a mad Indian Army colonel, or like the falcon Cully in T. H. White's novel *The Once and Future King*: 'His poor, mad, brooding eyes glared in the moonlight, shone against the persecuted darkness of his scowling brow.' (*A la recherche du temps perdu* is not my favourite book; *The Once and Future King* is.) Frequent experiences of finding himself out of his body had persuaded Bennett that there was more to the universe than the conventional understanding allowed. He had met Gurdjieff in Istanbul after the First World War and eventually he was appointed to be his deputy in Britain and later his literary executor.

Late in life he successively indiscriminately embraced Subud, Transcendental Meditation, Idries Shah's version of Sufism and, ultimately, Catholicism.

Some of my contemporaries followed the fat, baby-faced Meher Baba; others Bhagwan Shree Rajneesh, who collected Rolls-Royces and established a short-lived permissive commune in Oregon. Others again went into Subud, which sounded rather strange and violent. Various Sufi groups established themselves in Britain. Fayzal Inayat Khan was one of the many frauds to be found in London around this time. Idries Shah's form of Sufism did not seem to have anything particular to do with Islam. On the other hand, the Darqawi group, which had formed a commune in Maida Vale under the leadership of Ian Dallas, seemed admirably strict in its observation of all the ritual demands of Islam. Later I also visited Reshad Feild at the Beshara Centre in Swyre Farm in Aldsworth. Feild had been initiated by Pir Vilayat Inayat Khan but had also studied with Ali Bulent.

Earlier I promised that I would relate the end of Frithjof Schuon and warned that it was not good. As the decades passed he spent large amounts of time in the United States and his version of Sufism was increasingly centred around himself as a divine incarnation. Islamic rituals were sometimes replaced by Native American ones, with lots of drumming and chanting. There were 'primordial' dances in which the women were mostly naked and the men wore loin cloths. In 1991 a former follower denounced him, the police were called in and Schuon was indicted by a grand jury for child molesting and sexual battery though the case was eventually abandoned for lack of evidence. He returned to Switzerland where he died in 1998.

Though I wished to return to the *Zawiya* in 1969, I was warned that it would be dangerous to visit the place at that time. There was a lot of fear in Mostaganem. Twice the Shaikh had tried to leave the country, hoping to reach Paris or Brussels, but each time he was taken off the plane by the authorities. His health was never good and by now he was weakened by flu. Early in 1970 his twenty-year-old son Khaled, anticipating what was coming, fled the *Zawiya* and, despite being detained on the Moroccan frontier, eventually made his way to Casablanca and from there to Paris. Once he arrived in Ivry-sur-Seine, the *fuqara* assigned a bodyguard to protect him from the agents of the FLN. Other Mostaganese *fuqara* also arrived at the *Zawiya* in Ivry, including Abdullah Muslim and Sidi Said. Since the Ivry *Zawiya* found its numbers swollen by those who had fled Algeria, it had to expand into other houses in the neighbourhood.

A day or two after Khaled's flight the Direction Général de la Sûreté made its move against the *Zawiya* in Mostaganem and the Shaikh. Faid and Selima were arrested and taken to Algiers. There Saleh Vespa and his assistants in their bloodstained leather aprons were waiting for them. Saleh Vespa's real name was Saleh Hidjeb and I guess that he got the other name from a scooter he used to ride about in Paris. He was a Kabyle who first came to prominence as a racketeer in Paris, where he extorted protection money from cafés. Later he served with the FLN and I think that he was closely associated with Ali La Pointe, the protagonist of the Battle of Algiers. After the revolution, Vespa worked with Draia, the Chief of Police. Apart from being an expert in torture, he was also the regime's chosen hit man. For example, in 1970 he was dispatched to Frankfurt to murder the Kabyle Krim Belkacem, who had been one of the signatories of the Evian Accords with France. There had been heightened security at Frankfurt airport that autumn because of the recent attempted hijacking by the Palestinian Leila Khaled and consequently Krim had had his gun taken from him by the security people at the airport. Soon afterwards he was strangled by Vespa in a Frankfurt hotel.

Over the years Vespa did well for himself and retired to Switzerland. It is alleged that when he died, in December 2008, he left his family $15 million.

Anyway, it was Vespa who oversaw the torture of Selima and Faid. Among other things they were hung upside down and bastinadoed on the soles of their feet. Given the mindset of the regime, Faid had looked very suspicious. He had settled in the *Zawiya* in 1962 and, if he had ever had any identity papers, he had lost them long ago. What would such a foreigner be doing in Algeria except spying? But the sheer evil of what was done, the torturing of this childlike old man, who yet was practically a saint, is hard to contemplate. The *fuqara* in Paris made representations to the French government, who in turn made covert diplomatic démarches to the Algerian regime and, without any publicity at all, Faid and Selima were repatriated to Paris in June 1970.

The Shaikh was imprisoned elsewhere and for a long time his whereabouts were not known. According to Khaled, the Shaikh succeeded in converting his chief jailer to Sufism and the 'Alawi *tariqa*. After five months the Shaikh was released to house arrest in Gijel, a town in eastern Algeria. (Mostaganem is in the west.) I am not clear whether he had been tortured or not. In addition to the arrests, Boumedienne's regime seized a lot of the *Zawiya*'s property, as well as documents which it hoped would prove to be incriminating. The *tariqa* was tediously and unimaginatively alleged to be working for the Zionists and the CIA. The investigation got nowhere and I heard that consequently senior officials, including the minister in the Department of *Habous* (which dealt with religious properties), were sacked. The subsequent incoming minister was an atheist, or at least a non-practising Muslim, but nevertheless a friend of the Shaikh's. Finally, the Shaikh was released, but his health was broken. The confiscated part of the *Zawiya* came to be regarded as a matter of historic folklore, for an Algerian tourist brochure recommended it as a place worth visiting, before adding that it had once belonged to a Shi'ite sect who worshipped their leader as God and practised magic.

What happened to the Shaikh, Faid and Selima should be seen in the wider context of what was happening in Algeria in the late twentieth century. In part, the *Zawiya* was the victim of the ruling regime's determination that there should be no civil society – that there should be no organisations, orders or clubs that were not under the control of the FLN. It was a form of fascism. But the regime, which was really a military junta fronted by what looked like a political party, the FLN, was also subject to other pressures which it could not altogether resist. Boumedienne had pursued an Arabisation programme that aimed at replacing French, the hated language of the colonialists, and at the same time extirpating the Berber language and culture. In the short term, this made the teaching of serious academic and technical subjects rather difficult. Moreover, it was widely unpopular because a lack of good French would be a disadvantage for those Algerians who were seeking employment in France and there were millions who, driven by economic desperation, were doing just that. Also, Boumedienne's policy was unpopular among the Berbers, who did not want to surrender either their own language or the French which might be their passport to employment in Europe. The language question was one of life or death and many people were killed in the language riots.

But the most dangerous aspect of the Arabisation policy was that, because after years of French colonialism there were not enough well-educated teachers of either standard or classical Arabic in the country, the regime had to import Arabic teachers from elsewhere. Large numbers of these teachers came from Egypt and many of them were members of the Muslim Brotherhood, eager to escape from the thrall of Egypt's secularist regime, and they disseminated their fundamentalist propaganda in Algeria. Other teachers came from Wahabi Saudi Arabia and they propagated a different but parallel version of fundamentalism. Both the Muslim Brotherhood and the Wahabis hated the Sufis and regarded them as heretics. Their adherents in Algeria linked up with the local *'ulama'* and pressed for the persecution of Sufis. Though the regime found it easy to give way to the fundamentalists on this, in the long run their own tenure of power was fatally compromised by these early accommodations with fanaticism.

Although I never returned to Mostaganem, I stayed attached to the *tariqa* for some years. One night in December 1969 I had a vainglorious dream in which I was riding across the fields towards Mostaganem so that I could attend a great dance. I greeted white-robed *fuqara* returning from work as I overtook them. The fields were full of the sound of the invocation of Allah. As I crossed the fields my spiritual presence grew. The horse that I was riding was transmuted into an angelic power. I became increasingly Christ-like. The power of my *baraka* had become too strong for the angelic horse to bear. So I dismounted and together the *fuqara* and I entered an octagonal temple where people were getting ready for the *'imara*. Well, I have lived with dreams for so long and dutifully recorded so many, but at the end of it all I am disillusioned. The dream is not only a liar, it is also an incompetent narrator. I cannot think of anything useful I have learned from dreams, or any instance in which a dream has served as a valuable inspiration.

I went over to the Paris *Zawiya* in Ivry-sur-Seine several times. The place was small and scruffy and I felt ill at ease there. In Paris reunions took place on Sundays. The *fuqara* were overwhelmingly working class, mostly steeplejacks and bricklayers, and there was a great deal of camaraderie among them. But, by their common consent, the real 'heat' was in Mostaganem. In Ivry I performed the *'imara* once more and went *melboos*. *Fuqara* on either side of me held me upright, but my head was swinging wildly from side to side and I was trying to scream, though no sound was coming out. The fit swiftly passed and I continued in the dance for three more rounds, but only as a kind of zombie sustained by my companions. Then I felt I had to withdraw. I was ashamed and brought low and Faid rubbed it in later, telling me that it was precisely at the moment one felt that one could not go on that one should continue. One should become a corpse carried along by the spirit of the dance. But I was afraid of that shouting black centre and going *melboos* was a sign that not all was well with me.

Faid never talked about what had happened to him in Algiers and, indeed, I did not learn about the horrors until many years later. At Ivry, Faid was one of the two cooks. Every Thursday evening he used to lock and bolt himself in the *Zawiya*'s kitchen, strip himself naked and, singing at the top of his voice, simultaneously clean the kitchen and perform the ritual ablutions. But it was in Paris that he realised that he was impotent and that he was no longer getting those fantastic erections in which he used to revel. He a started a translation of the Bible into Arabic, but soon abandoned it. I could not understand where Khaled and Faid were going. In Ivry I re-encountered Selima, but we were never friends. I was a dog with Faid, but Selima was a cat. I heard from another *faqir* that, when I had last been in Mostaganem, Selima had noticed that I was under a fantastic illusion and she had told the Shaikh this and it was for that reason I had had to undergo a process of purification (but what was that illusion?).

The *Zawiya* at Mostaganem can be seen in retrospect as enshrining a traditional world of ritual, simplicity and serenity – an oasis of spirituality within which life was going on very much as it had for centuries. But to see it that way would be rubbish – a mirage. The *Zawiya* was of its century, the twentieth, and it was a fiery battleground where the *fuqara* fought among themselves and only united against their numerous external enemies. The modern literature of spirituality tends to be upbeat and sugar sweet – laughing Buddhist monks, cherubic Indian gurus addicted to practical jokes, the safe achievement of inner serenity and the dispensation of many words of personal comfort that might sit well in *The Reader's Digest*. My story has not been so sweet. In real life there are shadows, spiritual failures and political horrors. (And, besides, I have recently noticed that serious treatises by medieval mystics are mostly about suffering and hardly at all about spiritual delight.)

Khaled's paternal grandfather was Shaikh Hadj Adda Bentounes. His great-grandfather on his mother's side was the Shaikh al-'Alawi. Harvey and I had met Khaled from time to time in Mostaganem when he was still a slightly shy schoolboy. He had studied the Qur'an from the age of four and, by the time he was fourteen, he was learning how to be a commentator on the holy book. But I first met him properly in Paris. He was then perhaps twenty-one. He was good-looking in a Grecian way and obviously intelligent. When I met him, he was studying the *I Ching* and reading thrillers and Arab socialist literature. Briefly in revolt from the *Zawiya* and its ethos, he had grown his hair long, donned a black leather jacket, married a French-woman and set up a little shop in Les Halles which sold Afghan jackets. At one stage he ordered me to act as his rep with various clothing outlets in Notting Hill and this I attempted, though I did not succeed in getting any orders. Faid used to visit Khaled's shop in Les Halles to deliver more of his *mudhakarat*.

Shema was available at some French tobacconists and I regularly restocked. *Shema* aside, Paris depressed me, for I was sensing my limitations. I was no longer questing for the

Single Big Truth. I wanted to settle for smaller truths. While I walked around Paris, I was thinking that if salvation is not for everyone, then what is it for? I had set out for Mostaganem in 1965 confident and idealistic. Now I had lost that confidence. I knew I was not up to the spiritual path and I had become cynical. Yet I took some comfort from a saying of the Shaikh that a *faqir* had quoted to me: 'No matter how much one ignores my commands, disobeys them and does the direct opposite, I am always with that *faqir*.'

It was, I think, late in 1970 that Khaled and two or three others came over to England on a rather strange mission. After a meal at an Indian restaurant, the Agra in Whitfield Street, we went on to a meeting with a Dr Ross, an expert in occult mysteries and who preached the need to transcend one's 'petty ego-consciousness' and to achieve the state of non-attachment. He had made contact with an English *faqira*. Among those present that evening were the Baron and Baroness de Pauli and Ellic Howe, a Freemason who had written about the Order of the Golden Dawn and other aspects of occultism. Ross and his entourage were expecting Khaled to be a 'proper' Sufi and tell them lots of teaching stories in the manner of Idries Shah – stories which encouraged the listener to think laterally. But Khaled spoke first about the love of Allah. Speaking in French, he began by saying that there were two types of Gnostic, there were those who knew Allah and those who knew themselves, and that the latter knew more than the former. The interpreter, provided by Ross, could not believe his ears. Khaled went on to speak of his spoilt life as a boy who was the son of a Shaikh. But since then, he said, everything had been stripped from him, including his name.

Khaled later remarked that Howe, sitting at his ease on the sofa, had looked at his watch and thought, 'In ten minutes time all these young people will be under my power.' But Howe's words and personality made no particular impression on us and, after he left, Ross, shaking with tension, sank to his knees in some kind of silent invocation and continued to shudder, while we whispered among ourselves. Indira, a friend who had come with us, got the giggles as she watched Ross straining to summon up some kind of psychic power. A sort of astral battle in the manner of the *Doctor Strange* comics was presumably supposed to be going on, but we were perfectly at our ease and unimpressed by these strange people. Afterwards Khaled summed it all up by saying, '*Il faut beaucoup de noir pour voire la lumière.*'

While Khaled was in London he sent me to seek out Martin Lings, who, at that time, was still Keeper of Oriental Books and Manuscripts at the British Museum. I waited just inside the entrance of the museum until he emerged from the Oriental Printed Books and Manuscripts Reading Room at closing time. By now he was a saintly looking, white-bearded figure. I accosted him and gave him Khaled's message. Would he agree to a meeting? With scarcely a moment's hesitation he said no. He seemed astonished that I knew who he was. He was to die, aged ninety-six, in May 2005. The obituaries were respectful and rightly so. He was pious, modest, learned and hard-working. But some of his ideas (such as the hidden spiritual messages in Shakespeare's plays) were cranky and some of his associates (such as Schuon) were even crankier. In books like *The Eleventh Hour* Lings delivered unattractive rants against the modern world. Yet *A Moslem Saint of the Twentieth Century* is an eloquent masterpiece.

During this visit, Khaled told me that it was because I was '*serré*' that I could not stand the Paris *Zawiya*, but he also implied that we in England were prey to all sorts of evil influences which the Paris *fuqara* were protected from. Khaled was anxious to set up a *zawiya* for the British *fuqara* in London, Oxford or Cambridge. He told a British *faqir* that 'Time is a sword'. He returned in 1972, if I remember rightly, and this time he brought a coach-load of *fuqara* with him. Khaled stayed in a hotel, but where was his following going to stay? I came under heavy pressure to provide them with a night's lodging. (Harvey wrote to me later saying that it was a classical way of testing me.) At that time I still had my tiny room in Waterloo, but mostly I was living with my then girlfriend on the top floor of a house in Regent Square in Bloomsbury that belonged to the well-known literary agent Michael Sissons. Since Michael habitually went away for long weekends in the country, I guessed that it would all right to put them up on the floor of his spacious living room. Unfortunately ... Michael cut short his long weekend and came back early the next morning to find twenty or more white-robed dervishes sleeping on the floor of his living room. I do not have the words to describe his fury, but he soon recovered his cool and only a little later he was very generous to me and my girlfriend.

On 24 April 1975 Shaikh Hadj al-Mehdi died aged only forty-seven (and I believe that my initiation died with him). He had been elected by the Council of Sages in 1952. Khaled turned up at the funeral in a black leather jacket. Immediately after the funeral the Council of Sages met and elected him as their new Shaikh. Although, in *La Fraternité en héritage: histoire d'une confrérie soufie*, a book written jointly with Bruno Solt, Khaled claimed to have been taken totally by surprise at the decision of the Sages, Harvey and I had known years earlier that Khaled was destined to be the next Shaikh. Faid and Selima had been confident that this would be the case. But the black leather jacket and long hair proved useful, for the Algerian authorities gave him to understand that they thought they could do business with someone who seemed as modern as he did. They told him that it had been his father's traditionalist attitudes that had been getting in the way.

25. Shaikh Khaled Bentounes, the present head of the 'Alawi order

Although Khaled frequently visits Mostaganem nowa-
days, his main base is in France, where he is a leading figure
in the Muslim community and an *interlocuteur valable*
with the French government. The government has been con-
sulting him since 1999 with, among other things, a view to
better integrating the Muslims in France. Khaled is keen on
dialogue with Christians. He has published several books
on Sufism in which he emphasises its universalist message.
The 'Alawi *tariqa* also publishes *Terres d'Europe*, a magazine that is a successor to *Les Amis de l'Islam*, and Khaled
founded the *Scouts Musulmans de France*. These days the
'Alawiya, which has tens of thousands of adherents, is perceived as a modernising order.

President Boumedienne died in 1978 of a mysterious
illness and he was succeeded as head of state by Colonel
Chadli Bendjedid. Thereafter the regime slowly abandoned

Boumedienne's programme of socialist revolution. By then the country was in a bad way and Algerians contemptuously referred to their government as '*houkoumat Mickey*' (Mickey Mouse government). Because of the corrupt and incompetent manner in which collectivisation had been carried out, Algeria, which under the French used to export food, now needed to import it. There was raging inflation and high unemployment. The aimless, unemployed young men one saw everywhere, leaning against walls or squatting on pavements, were known as '*hittistes*'. (*Ha'it* means wall in Arabic.) A rise in prices of foodstuffs and a shortage of housing led to strikes and widespread violent rioting in 1988 and pressure was mounting for more democracy. The Front Islamique du Salut, or FIS, was formed in September 1989. It regarded the 'heroic' war of liberation from France with utter contempt and it despised the secular leftist regime which that war had brought to power. FIS was also an enemy of Sufism and, among other things, denounced the practice of visiting shaikhs' tombs.

Ominously, in 1990 FIS won seats in local elections. Then in January 1992 national elections got under way. From the first ballot it looked as though FIS would win the election. Its leaders made no secret of the fact that, if they won the election, this would be the last election ever to be held in Algeria, as a permanent Islamic state would be established, for elections were an unIslamic innovation. Although FIS was fighting the election, it held that democracy was not sanctioned by the Qur'an. Therefore the army panicked and cancelled the election. They also deposed the relatively liberal Bendjedid in favour of a hardliner, Mohamed Boudiaf, who was assassinated later that year. A prolonged civil war now began. Numerous FIS members were arrested and some were executed.

But the Armée Islamique de Salvation, or AIS, the armed wing of FIS, continued to wage guerrilla war from bases which were mostly concealed in upland forests. This was a jihad in order to establish an Islamic regime in Algeria, which in turn would be the prelude to the restoration of the Caliphate throughout the Muslim lands, as it had been in the first century of Islam. Ali Belhadi, the vice-president of FIS, declared, 'There is no democracy because the only source of power is Allah through the Qur'an and not the people. If the people vote against the law of God this is nothing short of blasphemy. In this case it is necessary to kill the non-believers for the good reason that they wish to substitute their authority to that of Allah.' Not only was FIS anti-democratic, it was rabidly anti-Semitic and xeno-phobic. Besides attacking the army, the police and foreign-ers, it made a point of murdering intellectuals, journalists, actors, singers and unveiled women. From 1992 onwards an estimated 150,000 died in terrorist atrocities.

Although FIS and AIS now appear to have been defeated, the Groupe Islamique Armé, or GIA, continues to fight on. It too seeks to re-establish the Caliphate. It takes as its watchword a verse from the Qur'an: 'Fight them until there is no more discord, and the faith belongs entirely to God.' Christians have been a particular target, for strict Muslims do not accept the traditional and conventional view that Christians and Jews should be tolerated because they are 'People of the Book'. Those Jews who were not lynched had left for Israel some time ago and one does not hear a whisper about their right of return to Algeria. As for the Christians, in December 1994 four White Fathers at Tizi Ouzuo were murdered by the GIA, who were proud about their achievement. The 'Alawi *Zawiya* at Mostaganem had always enjoyed good and close ecumenical relations with the Cistercian Trappist monks at Tibrihine. Faid told me, 'The Christians are very close to us. But if those Christians went up to the ordinary Muslim in the street, they would find a mountain between them.' In 1996 the GIA got to these monks too. Their bodies were never recovered, though their severed heads turned up a couple of months later. It is difficult, very difficult indeed, to be loyal to a religion some of whose members take pride in such things and claim that what they have done is sanctioned by the Qur'an.

The war in the nineties was a murky business. There were several splits within the Islamicist groups and, as the bloody years passed, they spent increasing amounts of time fighting each other. There were a lot of internal executions. Also, there was a large overlap between the holy warriors and criminal gangs. Accounts of spectacular atrocities continued to come in, but their significance was muddied by rumours that some of the atrocities had actually been committed by the army in order to boost their role as defenders of the people against extremists. It seems fairly clear that the army had infiltrated the GIA and that some of the massacres of civilians were actually instigated by the army. Tens of thousands were killed and more were 'disappeared'. Those Islamist guerrillas still fighting claim to be linked to al-Qaeda. As I write, it is now much quieter than it has been, but the advice of the British Foreign Office is still to avoid Algeria unless your journey is necessary and, even so, some areas are seriously dangerous. In the course of writing this book, I would have liked to go back to Mostaganem to see what memories it might have stimulated, but I dared not. As I have grown older, I have become more cowardly. I think of Algeria as a beautiful country populated by saints and murderers.

Anyway, to get back to mysticism, after the death of Boumedienne and faced with the rise of the Salafist version of fundamentalist Islam and similar militant groups, the regime reversed its attitude to Sufism and in 1991 a national association of *zawiya*s was established, something that would have been unthinkable earlier. Sufis were now in the ideological front line against violent fundamentalism. In July 2009, for example, the *Zawiya* 'Alawiya in

Mostaganem, with the official approval and sponsorship of President Bouteflika, held a conference with seminars, lectures and sessions of chanting which was attended by some 5,000 people. The broad theme of this gathering was tolerance. The event also marked the hundredth anniversary of the establishment of the 'Alawi *tariqa*, as it was in 1909 that Ahmad al-'Alawi had succeeded Shaikh Buzidi and established his own order.

In 1992 Esther Freud (who was born in 1963) published *Hideous Kinky*, a novel set in the sixties with strong elements of autobiography. It is the story of a young woman's hippy odyssey in North Africa, seen through the eyes of a five-year-old child. An adventurous, resourceful, but somewhat scatty mother, in flight from England and respectability, takes her two daughters with her to Morocco. The older daughter pines for school and a steady routine, but the younger one is more open to new experiences. Leaving the older daughter with friends in Morocco, the mother takes the five-year-old with her as she goes off in search of Sufi enlightenment in Algeria. The place she ends up in is Mostaganem. 'A man came out to meet us. He had a wild red beard that submerged his face up to his eyes, and his mouth was a crescent when he smiled.' (That must be Abdullah Faid.) Esther describes what she remembers of a *wird*:

> The boys sat in the circle with the men and wore white skull caps like their fathers. Mum and I sat with the women in their everyday clothes. We sat in a separate group shielded by a curtain and sometimes the women joined in the praying and sometimes they didn't …
>
> Sheikh Bentounes breathed in deeply through his nose, pushing his stomach out under his soft white robes and then letting his voice turn into a song as he controlled his exhaling breath for minutes on end. The men and boys that faced

him joined in a chorus that rose to a violent crescendo and then sank to a sigh as row after row bent their heads to rest their faces on the ground, leaving a soft silence hanging in the air with no noise but the whisper of perspiration trickling down the walls.

While the mother seeks spiritual enlightenment, her daughter is merely bored and tries to practise walking on her hands. She is glad when they finally leave the place and she can secure more of her mother's attention.

By the time I read Esther Freud's novel, I found myself looking at Mostaganem through the wrong end of a telescope. Everything seemed very small and distant, for, in the course of the seventies, I had slowly lost contact with Mostaganem, Ivry and the *fuqara*.

Back in seventies London, about three years after she had dropped me, Ayesha got in touch again and we had a wary meeting. She told me that she had been feeling guilty about us, but that, since then, she had been suffering in a disastrous marriage as much and more than she had made me suffer. She said that I had never known her but had just adored her in total blindness. Moreover, I had not changed, for I was still hopelessly idealistic and threw myself head over heels in love with one girl after another. I gathered that she thought I had turned myself into a character from Durrell's *Alexandria Quartet*, a tetralogy which she remembered me raving about. (Well, there are worse novels to be a character in.) I guess that, since by then I was no longer interested in her, by that very fact, belatedly I became desirable to her – too late.

So there I was, a sixties person who had lived on into the seventies. By now I had lost touch with most of my strange Oxford friends. Also, if the Sufi path was an exam, then I failed it. The path I thought I was following petered out in a maze of goat tracks and I betrayed Faid's hopes for me, just as earlier I betrayed those of my Oxford tutors. Still I continued to experience '*la presse*': 'Fire! God of Abraham, and of Isaac, and of Jacob ... joy, peace!' as Pascal described it, though it now came unpredictably and much more rarely. Then, at the mundane, non-ecstatic, non-romantic level, after five years of research, I was not succeeding in finishing my Ph.D. and, indeed, I never finished it. Nor had I found any useful employment. So read my tale and marvel. It is a tale worthy to be graven on the corners of the eyes with a golden needle, but don't go down my route.

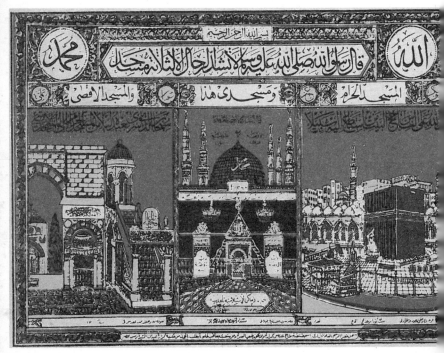

26. Mecca

LAST THINGS

AT THE END OF ROSE MACAULAY'S magnificent novel *The Towers of Trebizond*, Laurie, the narrator and protagonist, writes of her 'mortal fear and mortal grief' of dying, before continuing:

> After all, life for all its agonies of despair and loss and guilt, is exciting and beautiful, amusing and artful and endearing, full of liking and of love, at times a poem and a high adventure, at times noble and at times very gay; and whatever (if anything) is to come after it, we shall not have this life again.
>
> Still the towers of Trebizond, the fabled city, shimmer on a far horizon, gated and walled and held in a luminous enchantment. It seems that for me, and however much I must stand outside them, this must forever be. But at the city's heart lie the pattern and the hard core, and these I can never make my own: they are too far outside my range. The pattern should be easier, the core less hard.
>
> This seems, indeed, the eternal dilemma.

I wish that I had written that eloquent summation of spiritual failure. But how will this, my book, end? I am curious to know. Where do I stand? What does it all mean? My book was written in order to discover these things. At this late stage in my life, these are life and death questions for me – literally so, for when I die will I face examiners and, if so, how will I answer them?

Our pleasance heir is all vane glory,
This fals world is bot transitory,
The flesche is bruckle, the Fend is sle;
Timor mortis conturbat me.
>   (William Dunbar, *Lament for the Makaris*)

When I think a little more, there is also something else. As I get closer to death, it is natural for me to flee back in my imagination to my youth, to flee back to a time when I thought that I would live for ever. But now that I am old, I am, as Yeats put it, 'fastened to a dying animal'.

I first heard of the imminence of the Apocalypse and the coming of the Mahdi in the winter of 1964 as a young man in Oxford. Now, almost half a century later, these things have not happened. In every generation there are people who believe that they are living at the End of Time and that the rest of the world will come to a stop at around the same time that they do. But I no longer live in expectation of the Apocalypse.

A diary is a long letter written to the future self. It is now time for the future self to reply. My youth was simultaneously sweet and sad. It has been difficult to call it all back. If I had done the Proustian thing and had waited for involuntary memories to kick in and written just from them, then I would have a four-page memoir. Instead, I have had to struggle with skeletal memories, the reminiscences of friends and cryptic diary entries. The past, just by being the past, acquires a dubious poignancy. There is something unearned about the power of sepia photographs and of diary reports of parties attended by people who died long ago to move us. It seems as if youth was my proper home and it is that youth which I am homesick for. The passage of time weighs upon my heart. I have noticed this particularly when drifting off to sleep, when intellectual fences are down. According to Faid, 'One can never escape from the

Zawiya. Its influence always follows you.' And so it is that memories of that place have become my retirement home and I commune with the ghostly presences of the Algerian *fuqara*.

Memory is not a lumber room. It is constantly under reconstruction. Every morning when one wakes up, without being aware of it, one tells oneself a story about who one is – and over the years the story becomes refined, it changes and there is surely a danger that one's sense of identity comes to feed on things that never happened. It is tempting to think of my youth in the sixties as a *Bildungsroman*, which *Chambers Dictionary* defines as 'a novel concerning the early emotional or spiritual development or education of its hero'. But this is a memoir and not a novel, even though what I have written is not and cannot be the whole truth. I have left a great deal out that it would be embarrassing or dangerous to reveal, as well as a fair bit that would be merely boring. Since I respect their privacy, I have cut a number of people out of the narrative. Also my chronology may be occasionally confused. But I have made nothing up. I have told the truth … and nothing but the truth. No esoteric mysteries have been unveiled in this book. I did not understand what was going on in the sixties and I am no wiser now.

It would have been good for my salvation if it had been my destiny to become a holy fool. Unfortunately, I am the exact opposite and I find the Qur'an to be a problematic document – but then one would have to be an idiot not to find it to be a problematic document. For example, there are those mysterious letters placed at the head of certain *sura*s. Then there is the way some stories about prophets are told allusively. The text is self-contradictory in many places. Thus, according to *Sura 16, al-Nahl* (The Bee), wine is one of the blessings provided by God: 'And of the fruits of the palms and the vines, you take there from an intoxicant and a provision fair.' According to *Sura* 4, *al-Nisa* (Women), one should not pray when drunk, but, in *Sura* 5, *al-Ma'ida* (The Table), wine is denounced as an abomination devised by Satan and is forbidden to Muslims at all times. On the other hand, wine will be provided in Paradise. To deal with this kind of inconsistency, *naskh*, that is the science of determining which verses of the Qur'an abrogate other verses, has been elaborated over the centuries, but the doctrine of abrogation has been constructed on medieval premises and the chronology of Qur'anic revelation has not been established on a sound historical basis. Also, the membership of the audience to whom the Qur'an was revealed remains uncertain. Although I believe that the Qur'an contains profound and essential truths about God and his relationship with the world we live in, at the risk of seeming heretical, I do not believe that the Qur'an is co-eternal with God (and neither did the Mutazilites in the Abbasid period).

There are other problems with Islam. The following comes from *Sura* 4 of the Qur'an:

> *Men are the managers of the affairs of women*
> *For that God has preferred them in bounty*
> *One of them over another, and for that*
> *They have expended of their property.*
> *Righteous women are therefore obedient,*
> *Guarding the secret for God's guarding.*
> *And those you fear may be rebellious*
> *Admonish; banish them to their couches,*
> *And beat them …*

The text of the Qur'an, as we have it, seems to be explicit that women are not the equal of men and that they are to be beaten if they are disobedient. The Qur'an notwithstanding, I think that it would be shameful to hit a woman and, because of my Western upbringing, it does not seem right to me that in Islamic law a woman's testimony is regarded as having half the weight of that of a man. Back in the seventies Wansbrough told us in his class that there was actually no record of stoning for adultery ever having been carried out in Islamic history. Perhaps he was right then, but since his time hundreds of women have been stoned to death in Iran and there have been similar outrages in Afghanistan, Iraq and Somalia. I rollerblade regularly in Hyde Park and there it makes me angry when I see a woman veiled and dressed like a bin bag walking deferentially behind her Arab husband. Nowhere in the Qur'an is it decreed that women must cover their faces, nor is stoning for adultery enjoined by the Qur'an. But doubtless many Muslims will condemn me for failing to think myself free of the Western value system on this and other issues.

Clitoral circumcision and honour killings are certainly not intrinsic parts of Islam. Nevertheless, it is depressing that these things flourish mostly in Islamic countries. Slavery also continues in a secretive fashion in several Arab countries and, indeed, slavery seems to be sanctioned by the Qur'an. The corrupt brutality of such professedly Islamic regimes as the Saudi and the Iranian is not a good advertisement for the religion. The beheadings and amputations carried out by these regimes are abominable.

The hostility of so much of the Muslim world towards the West and Western culture is unattractive to someone who has grown up in that culture. It is dispiriting to learn that most Muslims reject Darwinian evolution. Hossein Nasr, one of the Perennialist authorities, has denounced the theory of evolution as an insidious ideology which is completely unscientific. According to Nasr, the theory must be wrong because it contradicts the Qur'an and *hadith*s. A person who espouses evolutionary theory cannot be a Muslim: 'The theory of evolution is the peg of the tent of modernism.'

The chilly legalism of the Muslim religious establishment is depressing, as is the petty ritualism. To take a very trivial example, I find the insertion by pious Muslim writers of the letters PBUH ('peace be upon him') after the Prophet's name, whenever he is mentioned in a text, to be unnecessary, perfunctory and typographically ugly. And, at the risk of being really shocking, I might ask why are most Muslims, Sufis apart, so boring? Why does their range of interests seem to be so narrow?

On the other hand, Islamic culture has many attractive qualities and over the years I have written a great deal about the literature and art produced by that culture. Historically, it has been a tolerant religion and one which to a large degree has adapted itself to local customs in India, South-East Asia, Africa and elsewhere. Moreover, for much of the Third World, Islam is the last line of defence against the sleazy values of the First World: the easy sex, the video games, the drunkenness in the streets, the cult of celebrities who are famous for being famous and the complacent belief in the triumph of the atheistic secularism of the West. Islam is an essentially democratic religion and it does not have a priesthood that holds a monopoly over the sacraments. A pure monotheism is surely easier to embrace than Christian doctrine and its complex acts of jugglery with the Trinity. Though often enigmatic, the Qur'an is a magnificent document full of profound truths, poetic imagery and driving rhythms. Moreover and much more importantly, I am conscious that in what I have written here, because of my limitations as a writer and for that matter as a person, I have not been able to get across the dignity, generosity and holiness of the dervishes with whom I spent my youth. Somehow it is difficult to write about sheer goodness. The practice of Islam is conducive to virtue and it has the power to fashion good people. Islam has a living and accessible mystical tradition. Doubtless such a thing exists in some

Christian circles, but it is harder to find. It is a long time since I have been in touch with the *fuqara*, but I admired them, for they were fantastic people, and some of the older *fuqara* in particular seemed to have been eaten away of all but holiness and gentleness.

Though Islam remains true for me, I cannot tell you why it should be true for you, and, besides, Faid told me, 'You must not say that you are a Muslim. You cannot know.' Fine. I cannot be dogmatic about anything, for the world is too mysterious. As Keats wrote: 'Negative Capability, that is, when a man is capable of being in uncertainties, mysteries, doubts, without any irritable reaching after fact and reason.' Not being able to say why Islam should be true for you, I have only tried to explain why it is true for me. I can imagine most of my readers saying, 'But you could not possibly have believed all that!' I could and I still do. I am incapable of denying what I experienced. But, even granting Islam to be essentially true, as I believe it to be, how does that solve the Meaning of Life? Frankly, I have no idea.

Wittgenstein wrote in the *Tractatus*, 'The solution to the riddle of life in space and time lies outside space and time', if that is any help. I believe in an afterlife, but this 'afterlife' so little resembles the life which it seems to follow on from that the word 'afterlife' may not be the right word to describe it. The afterlife does not follow life in roughly the same manner as après-ski follows ski or graduation follows exams, for after one's death time and space and everything else in the universe will be utterly different and utterly different in ways which it is impossible for us to imagine, for the universe is stranger than we can think.

I am averagely sinful, maybe even a little bit worse than average. *Video meliora proboque. Deteriora sequor.* (As with Ovid, I see the better and approve of it, but I follow the worse.) I found something encouraging in the writings of Archbishop Anthony Bloom, who was Exarch of the

Russian Patriarch in Western Europe: 'Ambrose of Optima, one of the last Russian Staretz, said two categories of men will attain salvation: those who sin and are strong enough to repent, and those who are too weak even to repent truly, but are prepared, patiently, humbly and gratefully, to bear all the weight of the consequences of their sins; in their humility they are acceptable to God.' Well, I hope so.

In Russell Hoban's wonderful children's novel *The Mouse and His Child*, a broken clockwork mouse and his son go on a prolonged quest to become self-winding. It was to be many years before I concluded my quest and became 'self-winding'. In the meantime I had so many teachers: Davis, Zachner, the Shaikh, Faid, Harvey; and there would be others in the future. Until I was well into my thirties I needed gurus. Also, as I aged, the world seemed to become more solid and less prone to revealing gaps and anomalies. It is no part of this memoir, but, in the long run, I felt the vast gravitational pull of the everyday, of work and of marriage. I fell to earth.

LIST OF
ILLUSTRATIONS

Illustration credits

3. Photo courtesy L'Association Internationale
Soufie Alâwiyya; 5. Photo Erich Lessing/akg-images;
6. Photo Casbah/Igor/Album/akg-images; 7. Photo c.1900,
Roger-Viollet/Topfoto; 10. Photo courtesy vitaminedz.
com; 25. copyright @ Catherine Touaibi, www.aisa-
suisse.ch

ACKNOWLEDGEMENTS

Helen Irwin, Juri Gabriel, Harvey, Andrew Topsfield, Bernardine Freud, Peter Carson and Mary Beard. All quotations from the Qur'an are from Arthur J. Arberry's, *The Koran Interpreted* (Oxford University Press, 1964).

Extract of 'Ash Wednesday' taken from *Collected Poems 1909–62 by T. S. Eliot* and extract from 'Little Gidding' published in *Four Quartets* ©The Estate of T. S. Eliot and reproduced by permission of Faber and Faber Ltd. Extract of 'Sailing to Byzantium' taken from *The Collected Poems of W. B. Yeats* and extract from *The Land of Hearts Desire* by W. B. Yeats reproduced by permission of A. P. Watt Ltd on behalf of Gráinne Yeats.